# 1 MONTH OF
# FREE
# READING

## at
## www.ForgottenBooks.com

By purchasing this book you are eligible for one month membership to ForgottenBooks.com, giving you unlimited access to our entire collection of over 1,000,000 titles via our web site and mobile apps.

To claim your free month visit: www.forgottenbooks.com/free559076

ISBN 978-0-483-60097-3
PIBN 10559076

This book is a reproduction of an important historical work. Forgotten Books uses
state-of-the-art technology to digitally reconstruct the work, preserving the original format
whilst repairing imperfections present in the aged copy. In rare cases, an imperfection in
the original, such as a blemish or missing page, may be replicated in our edition. We do,
however, repair the vast majority of imperfections successfully; any imperfections that
remain are intentionally left to preserve the state of such historical works.

# LINK

YOU'VE GOT TO RUN RISKS

NOTES FROM UPPSALA

MAN WITHOUT A ROAD MAP

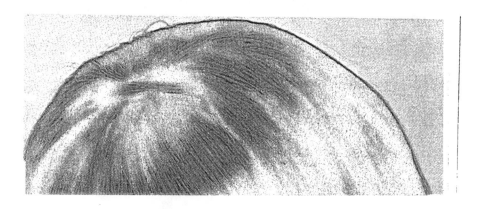

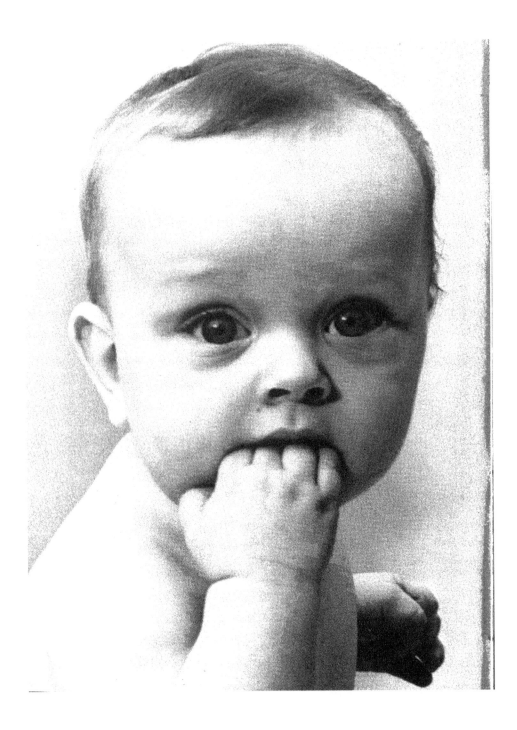

A PROTESTANT MAGAZINE FOR ARMED FORCES PERSONNEL

VOL. 27 • JANUARY 1969 • NO. 1

COVERS
    Front: "A New Year's gift to the world"....Photo by H. Armstrong
    Roberts.
    Back: Marking the Calendar. Photo by H. Armstrong Roberts.
    Inside Front: The fascination of the new—New Year, new child, new life.
    ...Eastern Photo Service.
    Inside Back: Friendship's Brand. Photo by H. Armstrong Roberts.

ART WORK: Illustrations by James Talone.

# SOUND OFF

**Why?**

Your article in the July LINK, "Can a Christian Participate in Killing?" was provocative as well as nearly absurd. Yes, we, through our neglect, are day by day allowing people to die but why should we multiply our sins by training for actively participating in intentional and deliberate killing of the most sacred thing on earth, the life of one of God's children.

—Greg Morse, US 56936707. E-5-1. USATC. Fort Lewis, Washington.

**Pen Pal Wanted**

The following letter from Canada was forwarded to us by the editors of *Christian Herald*:

I am a 16-year-old girl who wishes to correspond with an American soldier in Vietnam. Since some of your magazines probably reach the young boys there, I was hoping you might help me find a willing soldier for a pen pal. Write: Miss Grace J. Huizen, 77 Martin Ave., Winnipeg 5, Manitoba.

**A Letter from our Namesake**

Thank you for copies of THE LINK for July which I received about two weeks ago. I have been to Sidney, Australia, on a one-week R & R. For your information I have been promoted to another position since 11th of March. I am the information officer for a new support command—the Da Nang Support Command.... People in

*(Continued on page 65)*

## STAFF

Executive Editor ........................A. RAY APPELQUIST

Editor ..........................LAWRENCE P. FITZGERALD

Assistant Editor..............................IRENE MURRAY

Circulation Manager.......................ISABEL R. SENAR

Individual subscriptions: $3.00 a year. To Churches: $2.50 in lots of ten or more to one address.

For chaplains: Bulk orders to bases for distribution to personnel (in person, by mail, in back of chapel, etc.) invoiced quarterly at fifteen cents per copy.

Published monthly by The General Commission on Chaplains and Armed Forces Personnel at 122 Maryland Avenue, N.E., Washington, D.C. 20002.

Second-class postage paid at Washington, D.C. and at additional mailing offices.

Send notification of Change of Address and all other correspondence to Lawrence P. Fitzgerald, Editor, 122 Maryland Ave., N.E., Washington, D.C. 20002.

All scripture quotations, unless otherwise designated, are from the Revised Standard Version of the Bible.

4

# You've Got to Run Risks

By Thomas E. Moye

IT'S BETTER to be safe than sorry—who among us has not repeated those words with all the assurance of someone giving voice to incontrovertible, divinely ordained truth? It's better to be safe than sorry—who can argue with that? It seems so true, so self-evident, so inevitable.

But *is* it better to be safe than sorry? Oh, it's better to be reasonable and to exercise due care than to be foolish and rash. No argument there. But can you imagine some set of circumstances in which it might be better to be sorry than safe? You can't answer without first coming to grips with what is most important to you, with your scale of values. So the prior question is this: Is safety the highest good, the chief value and goal of life, and is risk the chief evil?

## Maybe It's Better To Be Sorry Than Safe

Try it out for a moment, just to taste the strange tang of it and to see if it fits any part of our lives— *it's better to be sorry than safe.* Well, it doesn't fit every part of life but the more we think of it, the more it does seem to fit certain important parts of our lives, parts that are inevitably loaded with risk. Every time you trust someone, every time you love someone, every time you call a man, "friend," you risk disappointment, betrayal, regret. Every time you embark upon any venture that is truly important to you, you risk failure with all its bitterness.

And yet, more lives of accomplishment and goodness and value are devoured by the counsels of a soft and frightened caution than by

CDR Moye is on the Staff at the U.S. Naval Chaplains School, Newport, R.I. 02840 overt appeals to greed and cruelty and godlessness. You don't have to be actually greedy—all it takes is to be afraid to risk being generous. You don't have to be actually cruel—all it takes is to avoid the risks involved in being kind to people. You don't have to be an atheist—all it takes is to refuse to trust in God. "I can't be bothered;" we say, "I don't want to get involved." And it's all variations on this single theme: It's better to be safe than sorry, and our whole lives and all our striving and every hope we cherish have boiled down at last to this weak and pallid residue: Safety means more than anything else to me.

Looked at in this light, we can begin to see what Emerson was getting at in his poem entitled "Sacrifice":

Though love repine, and reason chafe,
There came a voice without reply,—
"'Tis Man's perdition to be safe,
When for the truth he ought to die."

So safety, that glittering prize and paradise and haven toward which so many strive, now is perdition—and perdition is hell.

## Run Risks for What?

Disraeli said that "Youth is a blunder; Manhood a Struggle; Old Age a regret." Maybe so, but a great part of the regret a man may have at the end of his life will not be so much for the blunders and the struggles as for the times he failed even to try, to venture, to risk something, because he drew back from challenge and chose safety instead. It may be a bitter thing to look back

at last and say, I risked everything for love, everything for goodness, everything for the best I knew—and lost it all. But somehow that bitterness becomes illumined with a kind of glory when you compare it to this: I risked everything I had and everything I wanted to be for safety, and got it—and nothing else.

Shakespeare's words have more than merely romantic applications: "'Tis better to have loved and lost, than never to have loved at all." It can be better to be sorry than safe. It's better to have tried and failed, than never to have tried at all. It's better to have thrown all your resources in the struggle for some shining cause, and to have been bested, than to have stood off in perfect safety from the struggle of mankind.

Today mankind is involved in great struggles for justice, for decency, for peace, for freedom, against hunger and suffering and cruelty and oppression. No man ought ever to join in this struggle lightly and without realizing all that he is risking thereby. But he's got to make up his mind whether, above everything else in the world, he wants to play it safe, or whether he's going to put his life on the line for the kind of world he has seen shining, like the glory of God, in the face of Jesus Christ.

Wordsworth told us:

Give all thou canst; high Heaven rejects the lore of nicely-calculated less or more.

Nicely-calculated less or more—that's us, far too much of the time, figuring so carefully and precisely just how little we can risk, how little of ourselves we can commit to God and to mankind. We dole our lives out in such little pieces, such tiny amounts, such trivial commitments, because, after all, you know, it's better to be safe than sorry.

## Challenge to Lose Your Life

But Wordsworth said that high heaven rejects this kind of thing, and Jesus said so, too. Jesus put it this way: "For whoever would save his life will lose it; and whoever loses his life for my sake and the gospel's will save it" (Mk. 8:35). Is this a kind of glorification of failure and suicide? Of course not—this is just to say: You've got to run risks. If your life is ever to break out of the chains of mediocrity and failure, you've got to run some risks, you've got to stop being stingy with your life and begin to give it without reservation to God and your fellowman.

If safety is your only goal, and if you are waiting only for lead-pipe cinches to come along, keep waiting and they will come all right—but when they do come, you'll see that they're still what they always were: just death and taxes, that's all. But if you want something more from life than that, you've got to run some risks and give your life in faith and trust to him who has been there before you and who says now, "Follow me."

It may seem at first to be an irreverent thought, but have you ever wondered at the risks God took when he put the race of men on this green and lovely earth and gave us the freedom to enjoy and possess it—or to ruin and destroy it? And what did Jesus risk when he died for people like us? Was it really worth his while, or do you think he should have said, It's better to be safe than sorry? Well, that's a question that only he can answer, and we have his answer: He knew exactly what he was doing when he laid down his life for us. "No one takes it from me, but I lay it down of my own accord" (John 10:18). It wasn't fate or circumstances or duty that wrenched that decision from him, but "who for the joy that was set before him endured the cross" (Heb. 12:2), and "emptied himself"—no nicely calculated less or more here—"and became obedient unto death. . . ." (Phil. 2:7-8).

But there is another question which we—and only we—can answer: In response to the grace of God displayed toward us in our creation and redemption in Christ, what are we going to risk? Nicely calculated bits of less or more? Doling out the scarce and parsimonious crumbs of our lives, while we play it safe lest we be sorry? Or do we dare to bring to him in the arms of our faith all our hopes and dreams and fears and all we have and all we are, saying, "Here, Lord —this is Yours," ready to run every risk there is in this cause than to be safe in any other? ■■

If you must cry over spilled milk, condense it—F. G. Kernan.

# GALLANT YOUNG MEN
## and Their Sledding Machines

### By Lee MacDonald

TERRY Frazier went whizzing by on his Ski-Sled. His hands were above his head in a "look man, no hands" gesture. He was Ski-Sledding at Arapahoe Basin Ski Area west of Denver, where sledding isn't allowed.

However, this was an exception. Most ski areas, particularly those on U.S. Forest Service land, prohibit sledding, tobogganing and tubing, unless a special area is set aside for such activities.

But at A-Basin, particularly on Wednesdays since February, an exception to the hard and fast rule against sleds has not only been commendable, but logical.

The special sled is not the familiar steel runner version familiar to most people. It is a Ski-Sled.

The special people for whom the sledding exception is made are Vietnam veterans, now stationed at Fitzsimons General Hospital in Denver. Usually on Wednesdays you can find from two to six from that Army facility riding the chair-

lift and on the ski trails with the Ski-Sleds.

Two of the GIs are regular sledders at A-Basin—Terry Frazier, 21, of 5658 South Forest Hill, Littleton, Colorado, and Leonard Sparks, Jr., also 21, of 701 Claypool Rd., Muncie, Indiana. Frazier spent 10½ months in Vietnam with the 101st Airborne and Sparks was with the 4th Infantry for two months and two weeks.

Both would have much preferred completing their Vietnam tours for that would have meant each returned home with both legs. Frazier and Sparks are bi-lateral amputees.

Each Wednesday a bus from Fitzsimons transports a group from the Orthopedic Surgery Section to A-Basin. These are a special group of amputees, who lost a foot, leg, arm, or hand in the conflict in Southeast Asia, enrolled in the Amputee Ski School at the ski area. The bi-lateral amputees—those who lost portions of both legs—are not

8

Two gallant young Vietvets from Fitzsimmons Hospital ski-sled in the beautiful Arapahoe Basin west of Denver. Center is Leonard Sparks, Jr.; right is Terry Frazier. At left is an unnamed amputee skier.

able to attempt skiing. But they, and several other single amputees, can certainly Ski-Sled.

The Ski-Sled is manufactured by the Ski-Sled Corporation, 6515 West Grand Ave., Chicago, Illinois.

The sled consists of two wooden skis about four-feet long, a fiberglas, molded seat, a hardbrake mechanism, and a unique ball-joint hinged frame construction that permits independent movement of either or both skis. The skis also have a tremendous amount of side-camber, which enables the sled to carve a turn. A low center of gravity makes the sled difficult to tip over.

The amputee sledders have become very proficient with the Ski-Sleds, in fact, they are almost totally independent of help, except for a tow up the incline to get onto the chairlift.

At first a ski patrolman went along to pull the sleds and sledders across the flat areas, but the expert sledders, like Frazier and Sparks, figured out a way to manage the chore by themselves.

To move across the flat area near the off-landing ramp to the top of the ski trails requires an ingenious maneuver. The sledders line up their sleds side by side and by alternately pushing one sled and pulling another the line moves across the flat, like a sidewinder snake, until the pitch of the slope takes over.

The sledders ride the chairlift to midway and from that area navigate down the beginner-intermediate slopes and trails to the base area. It is necessary to stop the chairlift to load the sledders and sleds, but getting off requires just a momentary stop. The sleds are plopped down onto the ramp; the sledders bail out of the chairs onto the fiberglas molded seat of the sled and away they go.

Turning the Ski-Sled is done by shifting the weight from right to left by leaning. The sled turns in the direction the rider leans as the skis are edged into the snow.

What about spills?

"Oh, sure, we take a few now and then," says Frazier, "particularly when we run into several moguls (bumps). The moguls sometimes spin us around and the back tips of the skis dig in tossing us out. But spills are all part of the fun."

The skiing and ski sledding for the amputees has done much for their morale and psychological well-being. It has also done some good for hundreds of sound healthy skiers at Arapahoe Basin, who are prone to complain occasionally about conditions or other skiers.

Complaints have suddenly diminished, particularly on Wednesdays when the amputees are there. There just doesn't seem to be any foundation for the usual complaints.

Another very important aspect of the ski and ski-sled amputee program is that the other skiers and spectators at the ski area soon realize these gallant young men are not handicapped. They only seem to have a complication which desire and determination are rapidly overcoming. ■ ■

### ATONEMENT

Here is all you must do:
take the blank page
of your tomorrows and
as if it were a contract

sign your name at the bottom

and give it to God;
then set forth confidently
trusting him to write your life
in his hand.

—Pollyanna Sedziol

# How My Faith Has Helped Me in the Military

FOR FIVE years I have been a Christian, and three of these years have been spent in the U. S. Air Force. Because of my travels, I have met in fellowship with many Christians, both military and civilian. It is wonderful to know that Christ is preached throughout the world, even here in Vietnam.

I have had the privilege of meeting missionaries from New Zealand and Australia, working here with the Vietnamese. It is a great sacrifice for Christians to leave their homes to tell others of Christ's love. My heart goes out to these people who are willing to leave their loved ones in order to work for Christ.

Praise the Lord for full-time Christians. Too many of us are satisfied to be part-time Christians. How can we expect to be able to witness to His glory if we become Christians only on Sunday?

A correspondence course led me to our Lord. A "Gospel Bomb," a roll of Bible tracts, plus the course itself, were thrown from a car, picked up by a friend, and given to me. I began the course, and before completion, a saving knowledge of our Lord was received and believed in my heart. I began a personal correspondence with Pastor Ney whose course I had taken. We have corresponded these five years. Only last year, several weeks before I came over here, we finally met and I was baptized. Pastor Ney's letters and tape-recordings continue to be a blessing to me. I am looking forward to meeting him again when my tour of duty is over.

As each day passes, my faith increases, and I grow stronger in the Lord. Reading God's Word, praying to Him, singing in praise, and telling others of His love, are leading elements in my life. If we do not enjoy these things now, how can we expect to enjoy them for eternity?

—A2C **Clyde W. Moyer**

(Address: CMR #1, Box 374, 637 SVS. SQ. APO San Francisco 96316.)

# Cry for Life

## By Warren Wilder

### An incident of hard-to-believe viciousness

"JUMP! Jump! You fool, jump!" With astonishment Corporal Joe Ramsey listened to the savage cries of the crowd. Men and boys of all ages eagerly urging the man on the ledge to leap to his death.

It was a cold, oppressive day, windy, with dark swollen clouds gathering in the west. The soldier found himself chilled, shivering after standing for several minutes at the edge of the crowd.

The chant went up again.

"Jump! Jump!"

Incredibly they were taunting, even daring the poor miserable man above to end his ordeal, to bring down the curtain on whatever crisis had pushed him so far.

Ramsey felt curious about the man on the ledge. He looked forlorn and lost. In the gray fog that distorted the buildings, the man appeared as a leaf in a storm, trampled and defeated.

The crowd was swarming on the pavement below the seven-story red brick building. The object of their taunts was a young man poised on a small ledge just outside the window of the top story. He stood very quietly, looking down, occasionally bending a little like a diver about to plunge into deep water.

Ramsey, a former reporter before enlisting in the service, felt a desperate urge to get the facts. Who was the man? Why was he threatening to jump?

At the back of his mind another thought stirred: Why, after all, should he become involved? After sweating out a year in the muck and mud of Vietnam, he needed a glorious dose of R and R. He wanted to fill every moment of his holiday, every hour with the incredible joy of living. He'd looked forward to returning stateside. Now, ironically,

12

he was watching a civilian who'd probably never seen service or tasted the hell of combat threatening to kill himself.

Distraught, Ramsey looked around searching for a familiar face. This was his hometown, his neighborhood. There must be someone he knew.

A face, familiar which he couldn't recognize caught Ramsey's eye. He pushed through the crowd toward a man staring up detached, but perhaps more sympathetic than those around him.

He said loudly: "Don't I know you?"

He was relieved to see the man break into a wide grin and put out his hand. "Why, hello, Ramsey, sure you know me. I'm Fred Silvers."

Ramsey nodded.

"Where you been so long, old buddy?"

"Doing a hitch with Uncle Sam."

"Been to Vietnam?"

He nodded slightly, vexed over the next question which would come automatically, not wanting to discuss the matter. And yet, when the question came, though Ramsey's face turned bitter, he didn't hedge. "You want to know what it's like over there? You wouldn't believe it if I told you. You have no idea..."

"No, I guess not," the other agreed.

But he was staring upwards and Ramsey, following his gaze, asked: "Who is he? Do you know?"

"Oh, some salesman with family trouble. Must be very bad. He's

14

been up there over an hour. And this pack of vultures here," Silvers gestured accusingly at the crowd, "has been egging him on all that time."

Ramsey felt his temper rising and the cords in his neck tighten with anger. "Why doesn't someone try to help?"

"They did," said Silvers. "A policeman went up there. This crazy joe threatened him with a gun. Said he'd kill him if he didn't leave him alone. They're trying!"

Ramsey shook his head sadly, and the restlessness of the faces was starting to gnaw on him. He felt sick and disgusted. "Jump! Jump!" The cry had settled into a rhythm. When he left Vietnam, he thought he was returning to civilization. Now he wondered about that, too.

With a shrug, Ramsey moved out from the center of the crowd, angry with himself for having lingered so long. In recent months he'd been soaked with man's inhumanity to man. Who needs this show? Who needs any further reminders?

YET as he walked away, Ramsey felt troubled, not so much from the crowd's reaction, as from his retreat.

Not that he was a coward. No one had ever accused him of that. It was just that he was haunted by the memory of a night in Vietnam, when a selfish act of his—some minor thing that he'd discarded completely until he was reminded of it—had put him to task.

Ramsey's best buddy had pointed out the nature of his trouble. Even now, as he drew further away from the crowd, his buddy's words still taunted him: "Ramsey, I'm going to tell you one thing. It's gonna hurt. But I've watched you for a long time now and, damn it, you're selfish! You know that? You care for nobody but yourself. That's your whole trouble, you really don't care for anyone..."

The words had stunned him then and they still hurt. No one had ever struck him so hard.

And the more Corporal Ramsey thought about it, the more it worried him. Later, it became like something eating away inside him; a voice like the enemy crying inside, which couldn't be silenced.

Why should it bother him so? He would never know, but it did. Now, it seemed, it was eating away at him stronger than ever.

It shamed him, and it made him angry. On this gray January morning, with black clouds looming overhead, he had a chance to prove he wasn't a ruthless egotist with no regard for his fellowman. Of course, he'd have to go back to the crowd no matter how great the risk. The man on the ledge was struggling for life, and in these last few minutes maybe a bystander's wisdom might make the difference.

Ramsey did a rapid about-face. Somehow, he thought, as he bumped against people, he would have to instill in one wretched human being the will to survive. Maybe impossible, but he'd try.

As he started inside the building, a long shrill cry rose in the center of the crowd. And the craning of necks, the tension in faces told Ramsey there might be considerably less time than he'd thought. He said to a policeman, "Let me try!"

He prayed that the young man wouldn't leap before he had a chance to speak to him. What a rotten finish that would be!

He leaped up the steps of the winding stairway two at a time. Anxiety pounded in his ribs. Hold it, kid; hold it, kid, he was thinking. And then he was saying it aloud, standing at a safe distance. "Hold it, fellow."

The other man's head jerked around and half of his long uneasy frame twisted through the open window. Ramsey saw the naked fear on the lean face, the frightful eyes peering at him in anguish.

"Move away!" he cried. "I'll jump!"

The young man turned toward the crowd. He pulled out a black revolver, but the sight of it failed to stir Ramsey. The young man was too awkward, too shaky to really scare the war veteran, though Ramsey felt tension as he stood watching him. You never knew what a nervous guy might do.

Forget the pistol, he told himself. Forget the absurd threats. What you've got to cope with is what's inside this guy. Show him you're not afraid. Stare and keep staring at the black metal, and try to think of this man's misery, the terrible agony he must have suffered before he came to this moment.

He tried to look into the man's eyes as he turned toward him. It was like gaping into the eye of a hurricane from the vantage of a cockpit.

"I said go away!" the man threatened. "Did you hear me!"

When he saw that Ramsey wasn't obeying his order, he grew confused. His face reddened. "Listen to me, I said get out of here. Do you hear? Leave me to die in peace!"

But Ramsey didn't budge. "Stop waving that pistol," he said. "Put it down." His voice was cool, hard.

Disconcerted, the young man screamed. "You don't have to die, too! If you want to live, take my advice and get out of here!"

Ramsey waited quietly: "I'm not going anywhere."

The young man sneered. "What makes you so brave?"

"What makes you so cowardly?" replied Ramsey. "Because that's what you are."

He gave Ramsey a long bitter glance. "You don't know anything." Then he stared out of the window, saw that the sky was wild with the threat of wind and rain. The crowd huddled together. "And down there, they don't understand anything either."

"Perhaps not." Ramsey looked down. Like an ugly inkspot on the pavement, he thought and shuddered.

Then in the pause he tried to size up the situation. He could either take the fellow by force or remain here, maybe for hours, attempting to reason. The latter alternative gave him a feeling of frustration. He wasn't a psychiatrist. He couldn't put this man on a couch when he was teetering on a ledge

seven stories up.

IF ONLY the jeers of the crowd would cease long enough for him to think! The crowd was having an unsettling effect on him. They were enough to make anyone want to jump. He was surprised the young man had held on for so long.

"Jump! Come on, jump!" Ramsey heard. "We haven't got all day!"

Ramsey's tongue flicked out. He licked his upper lip bitterly. And he saw the young man stiffen.

"Don't let them bug you, fellow."

With puzzled, hunted eyes like a wild animal trapped in the forest, he gazed at the soldier. "They," and his lips trembled slightly, "they want to see me die."

The soldier waited a moment and said compassionately: "I want to see you live."

The young man, still gazing at him, clung to these last words with child-like disbelief. For a moment his lips tightened, his eyes trying to understand.

Gradually the crowd melted away under a sudden shower, wind lashing the rain furiously. The young man gave Ramsey a hint of his difficulty. By this time the revolver was back in his pocket.

"When I came home the other night," he began, "I found my wife sitting quietly in our bedroom sewing. Then I heard her say, 'I want a divorce.'"

He paused to see if Ramsey heard. He went on.

"I thought we were getting along fine. But she's already got a lawyer, started proceedings without telling

16

me. Have you ever been hit with a hammer?"

"No, not that kind," Ramsey said.

"I walked the streets all night, remembering how it was before I met her. I thought of my two boys. I saw everything I'd built up in five years of marriage suddenly bombing out. She couldn't do this, I said. And yet, she was. She said she loved someone else. Can you imagine that?" In his agony the young man's eyes opened wide. "It happened just like that—just like that." He snapped his fingers.

"So you think you've got a right to come up here and make a show of your misery? Is that it? You think you're the only man who's ever had a run of rotten luck? How will that solve your problem?"

"It'll end my problem."

"Maybe I'm not getting through to you. But let me say this. You're going through hell, maybe, but you're not the only one. Every day, every minute, someone is being dealt a savage blow. Is this the first time anything like this has ever happened to you?"

The young man's face darkened with the bitter memory of rejection. "The first time."

"Then you're lucky. Most people have more than one crisis. So this is your first. Only the way you're facing it doesn't make sense."

"I know it doesn't. I'm ashamed, but..." His face was torn. "I couldn't—I couldn't think of any other way."

For a long while Ramsey watched him. "How about your boys? They'll be real proud of you."

The accusation of his Vietnam buddy still haunted Ramsey. If his buddy were here now, he'd have to admit he'd stuck his neck out for someone else. He cared what happened. He thought of his buddy for a moment. Maybe he'd been using a little psychology on him, seeing that Ramsey was down in the dumps himself. And by making him mad and challenging him, he'd pulled him up short.

Still thinking about it, Corporal Ramsey turned to the man. His eyes were not as sympathetic as before. "Listen to me, fellow, you can make me out a filthy liar if you want to, but, personally I hope you've got the guts to see this thing through. I honestly hope you've got what it takes to face up. Tell me, right or wrong?"

Ramsey's eyes blazed at him, filled with a strong steady light of hope. "How about it? Let's go, fellow. Let's get out of here. Everyone's washed out with the rain." He gave a low chuckle, then advanced several steps toward the young man, his heart hammering for fear his movements would be repelled, causing the man to leap in a final futile gesture.

But in one more moment he'd know; it would have to end somehow. Ramsey advanced further, slowly, groping for another moment in which to dissuade him. "Listen to me," he said quietly, "hold it fellow, there, easy now." Then his arm stretched out, his strong fingers were resting on the fellow's shoulder. The young man didn't as much as

17

flinch; he was as calm as the storm outside was violent. And then Ramsey gulped with thanks.

"Come on, let's have a cup of coffee."

The uneven breathing of the young man was the only thing that remained of his suicide threat. "Coming with me?" Ramsey asked impatiently. "We'll flip to see who buys."

When the man leaped down into the room, Ramsey felt relieved! Together they stepped into the driving rain and ran for the diner across the street. ■■

# Lines from the U.S.A.

### By Eva Kraus

GOOD SAMARITAN...For three years Mrs. Angela Romelli from Germantown, Pa., has been scanning lost and found columns of some half-dozen newspapers for news of lost and found dogs. She matches the owners to the lost dogs, and has now founded the Lost Pets Society with 50 members assisting her in this avocation.

HAPPY ANNIVERSARY...Mr. and Mrs. George B. Webb of Suffield, Ohio, have been married 65 years. At their anniversary party when asked to what they attributed their happy marriage, the 1903 bride replied, "The most important thing is for one to stay out of sight when the other is upset."

CASH ON THE LINE...When the marriage license bureau in Denver began having checks received "bounce," they passed a new rule: only cash accepted for licenses.

SAVED BY THE BELL...Mrs. Sarah Mann of Knoxville, Tenn., owes her life to a bell. Fire in her attic burned a wire leading to her doorbell which rang until she was awakened, thereby saving herself and four children.

COMFORT AND CONVENIENCE...When motorists in Milwaukee break the law, they can pay fines in comfort and convenience. Drive-in windows have been installed for violators who can pay their fines without getting out of their cars.

LUNCH ON THE HOUSE... In an attempt to get more depositors, the Waterbury (Conn.) National Bank now gives cream cheese sandwiches with each deposit.

IGNITION KEY
We might prevent the bitter tear
Which has so often stung,
If we would set the brain in gear
Before we start the tongue.
—Mary Hamlett Goodman

Among the 730 voting delegates representing 232 member churches at the 4th Assembly of the World Council of Churches in Uppsala, Sweden, were Archpriest Jerzy Klinger (left) and Metropolitan Stephan of the Orthodox Church of Poland.

# Notes from Uppsala

### By Herman N. Benner

REPORTERS, delegates, participants—they came from all over the world—from Africa, Asia, South and Latin America, North America, Europe, the Isles of the Pacific, Australia, Russia, India, Japan, Hong Kong, Southeast Asia. They came to Uppsala, Sweden, in July, 1968, for the 4th General Assembly of the World Council of Churches. They came 2,000 strong. The Iron Curtain was down; not so the Bamboo. No one was there from communist China.

The 3rd General Assembly had met in New Delhi, India, in 1961. During these past seven years miracles in the ecumenical cooperation of the churches have taken place.

19

One of the most important religious gatherings in 1968 was the 4th General Assembly of the World Council of Churches meeting at Uppsala, Sweden, 4-19 July. Chaplain Herman Benner of SHAPE served as an accredited correspondent for THE LINK and THE CHAPLAIN at Uppsala. We are happy to present in this article some notes and observations of Chaplain Benner who at SHAPE is already working in the midst of an international, interfaith, ecumenical Judeo-Christian center. Our correspondent was tremendously impressed with Uppsala. He writes: "Uppsala tied together a lot of forward-looking spiritual concepts with a sense of urgency which I have not felt elsewhere."

## The Challenge of One World

The Uppsala Cathedral is one of the most beautiful in the world, with its twin Gothic spires and interior high arched reaches. More plain is the ancient Uppsala Castle that served the old Vikings for victory banquets in the smorgasbord manner.

It was here on the eve of the Assembly that Dr. Eugene Carson Blake, General Secretary of the WCC, briefed several hundred of us press people on what to expect. He asked:

Can this assembly adopt a forward-looking program in today's new moral sense and approve a program as to how it is to best serve Christ today?...

The day of autocratic churches in Christendom is past both for the World Council of Churches and for the Roman Catholic Church... It is just possible that these sessions together may spark all the denominations here suddenly to see by the power of the Holy Spirit that the new style of life no longer permits the insulation and isolation of one Confession from another....

## The "Aged Ecclesiastics"

No longer can it be said that the World Council of Churches is only a Protestant body. Its largest component of churches comes from the Old Catholic Orthodox ranks. Looking at the colorful dress, the heavy long beards, the high fancy headgear, the swirling flowing robes, and the venerable years of many of these "aged ecclesiastics," as they were called by some, one wondered whether these Orthodox Patriarchs of the church did not more belong to Old Testament times than to the present. However, some of us were happily surprised to find that these prelates could do more than chant and swing incense. Some of the earliest and most articulate leaders of the ecumenical movement come from their churches. We soon found that some of the best thinking on the focus of Christendom today came from their midst.

## Uppsala's Backdrop

Uppsala was a marvelous demonstration of the churches seeking to use their diverse powers to serve

A colorful processional in Uppsala Cathedral during the opening of the 4th Assembly. Attending were King Gustaf Adolf VI and President Kenneth Kaunda of Zambia, who later addressed the Assembly. Leading the procession were officers of the World Council, the Executive Committee, and the Swedish Host Committee, who were followed by official delegates from over 200 member churches.

Dr. Barbara Ward (Lady Jackson), noted British economist, writer, and Roman Catholic laywoman, spoke on "Rich and Poor Nations" at the plenary session. In 1967, Lady Jackson was named Albert Schweitzer Professor of International Economic Development at Columbia University, New York City.

Christ in the world's seething turbulence today. Against a backdrop of the following agonizing tensions, the 3,000 delegates, participants, and observers worshiped, listened to experts, discussed, prayed, deliberated and took action.

Several massive student revolutions had just toppled a few governments and threatened more.

The war in Vietnam was on the top of everyone's mind.

An ugly civil war in Nigerian Africa was starving millions of desperate people.

Some scientists were predicting man's demise by atomic annihilation, and this within a generation.

The growing gulf between the rich and poor nations, between the "haves" and "have-nots" required some reversal now.

Author James Baldwin warned of impending black-white racial confrontation from Africa to the Atlantic Community that could soon become a conflagration.

The growing tensions between the generations threatened to sweep away loyalty and allegiance to traditional Christian values among the radical youth of today.

The steam of long developing liberal changes in the government of Czechoslovakia was putting pressure on the Russians.

Church leaders from all these areas of tension and turbulence were at Uppsala. Could one have great expectations of unified Christian action faced with the confrontation of head-on loyalty to tribal-regional points of view and ideologies? To say nothing of acrostic antagonisms and accumulated suspicions of one another from centuries of "religious wars?" Yet, here they were. Here in charity and amiability working in unity of spirit for man's salvation with reasonable selflessness. As the French would say: "Formidable!" (Unbelievable).

## The Growing Climate of Ecumenism

Could it "come off" at Uppsala? Dr. Blake had good reason to wonder. An ecumenical miracle had happened in the last twenty years. At Amsterdam in 1945 some 142 sovereign churches had come together to pledge to form the World Council of Churches. Since then the interfaith climate of ecumenism had grown. At New Delhi in 1961, much progress had been made, but the Orthodox churches felt they had to issue separate statements on each issue to make their voice heard. Not so at Uppsala. The New Delhi acclamation: "We accept afresh our calling to make visible our unity in Christ" had assisted the churches to develop in mutual trust and understanding, even across the political divisions and racial frustrations of modern man. The spirit of penitence, hope, and great expectations under the leadership of the Holy Spirit was evident among most delegates. The desire for solidarity in Christ and to express in humility the power of his church to prepare the way of his kingdom motivated many.

## Youth and Female Representation

With the memory of the Sorbonne uprising in France and the Columbia University take-over still fresh in mind, how did these "established" heads of churches respond toward the turbulence of today's youth? From Dr. Blake on down, it was made plain that the leadership of the WCC desired more not less youth participation. The Council had helped some 150 youth participants from all over the world to get to Uppsala, that they might have their guidance. "Club 68," the Christian Youth Center, served as the focal point for the voice of youth. Some alleged "professional youth" leaders of the far political left could not wait to whip up a condemnation statement against the United States on its involvement in Vietnam, which

they did. But on the more solid religious issues and application of Christianity to constructive guidance, their pronouncements were not as concerted, though a stimulant to the prelates.

By the time leaders become heads of churches they are normally well beyond age fifty. Thus with each denomination allotted only a few delegates, some only one, only the matured are qualified to represent a church. Therefore, youth leadership is not very much possible among the delegates.

The same problem applies to the ladies of the church. Few heads of churches are female because few denominations encourage or desire ladies to be part of the clergy.

## The Left Side of Cloud "9"

War in Vietnam and Biafra/Nigeria was never far from anyone's thinking, what with the Paris "peace" talks underway, and starving Biafrans pleading for assistance. The resolution on Vietnam said: "The mortal suffering of the Vietnamese people should at once be ended, with immediate and unconditional cessation of the United States bombing of North Vietnam, and all use of weapons of mass destruction." The resolution on Nigeria/Biafra made an urgent plea for both sides to end their hostilities and get together at the peace table.

On both these problems, action taken seemed a little like good advice poured from the left side of Cloud "9," imbedded in fanciful and wishful thinking, playing into

23

the hands of, but quite unable to redeem the gangsters internationally who are responsible for stealing, murdering the innocent, taking their countries and possessions and making of what life there is left a terror or a depressed nonentity of peasanthood and slavery. The change from fantasy to base-rock reality is so noticeable here in Europe after the brutal, crushing military occupation of Czechoslovakia by the Russians and satellites. Before, it was detente, rosy-eyed hopes for growing decency within Stalinist communism, and belittling NATO and the strength of the U.S., were common attitudes especially among the young who did not have burning memories of Hungary and East Berlin and the Cold War. Now the attitude is reversed in many areas. Such is human nature.

## The Security of All Nations

We were disturbed that so many of the churches of the world were ready to condemn the United States for being true to its pledge to help a friend in desperate trouble, while unwilling to condemn the terrorists who openly tell the world they are going to steal and plunder and take as many nations around the world as they can get away with. Why so one-sided? Appeasement toward the brute reality? Real pink sympathy on the part of many to encourage the "opposite" and see him dominate the earth until the four horsemen of the Apocalypse eschew us all? No willingness to learn from the lessons of history that such

vicious attempts at crass domination must be repulsed before they gain momentum? Would there be a different reaction now that the true nature of the "preempt" is again laid bare before the world?

Interestingly enough, the resolution on the Middle East declared: "The independence, territorial integrity, and security of all nations in the area must be guaranteed. Annexation by force must not be condoned." One wonders if they would have used as strong words in regard to Czechoslovakia. We hope so.

## The Good Samaritan's Touch

Such a Christian socialist economist as Dr. Barbara Ward, Albert Schweitzer professor of Economics at Columbia, and Lord Caradon, British representative to the United Nations, presented lucidly and forcibly the growing problem of the rich nations getting richer and the poor nations getting poorer progressively by the year 2000 A.D. They agreed that something must be done to reverse immediately the flow of wealth "to him that has." The President of Zambia in Africa told how disillusioned newly independent and underdeveloped nations are with their morass of poverty and inability to extricate themselves. The rich nations hold economic power and dominion by reason of their economic strength. The poor nations have to pay heavy interest rates, except at the World Bank which had only a limited amount of money to lend. Why not have all nations pay one to three

24

percent of the GNP (Gross National Product) into a fund to assist the developing nations to get onto their feet a little faster? There is a feeling of the rich not caring enough to render such assistance. The plea was made for all Christians to start a self-tax program of giving a percentage of their income to help the poor, as a start. Real compassion and desire to sacrifice for the "poor and helpless" had the warmth of the Good Samaritan's touch at Uppsala. A new appeal to the churches for a 3 million dollar goal for relief operations was approved. The "Third World" cried for help. The pleas of the poor and unfortunate were heard at Uppsala.

## Racism and Affluence

The issue of racism was never far from consciousness. In no place on this earth have so many who care so deeply for all men, who are grieved at man's racial prejudice and bias toward his own kind come together in penitence, prayer, and mutual helpfulness as at the 4th General Assembly of the World Council of Churches at Uppsala, called "Christianity's most representative gathering in the last thousand years of Christendom's history."

Racism and deprivation because of race were roundly denounced in all their heinous aspects. The motivations stirred up will continue to bear fruit "to the least of these" for years to come.

## The Generation Gap

In some ways the youth of today articulate the realizable goals of Christianity's task often without deep rooting in the message and mission of Christ per se. They reflect a deep impatience with theological verbalisms not first seen in action. Thus, they are labeled revolutionary. Dr. Theodore Gill, in charge of the educational phase of World Council relationships, gave one of the most lucid analyses of the student mind and soul today to the conferees.

Youth takes seriously man's idealistic possibilities and is no longer content to let entrenched economic and political power hold down man's latent humanity to man, he intimated. "Establishments" that have failed just repeat the old worn-out formulas of war, hate, lust and greed to get and keep for self. A secular type of Christianity demands what Christianity has been teaching for 2,000 years, to become a reality, now. The "old man" may not see how sharp this cleavage is. It is so sharp that modern left-wing youth are even disillusioned with Russian and Chinese communism which mouthed such utopian objectives and "bad-mouthed" humanity to death on the road to them.

The delegates of the Assembly tried to understand this unrest of today's generation and its dissatisfaction with yesterday's answers. The suggestion was made for a Christian Peace Corps to express in action the young generation's revolutionary desire to assist those who cry for human dignity, life, racial equality, liberty, economic adequacy and spiritual solvency before God through education and functional Christianity.

## The Direction of the Travel

We could comment on many aspects of the World Council's work, on many of the theological studies and depth analyses of application to our contemporary world. In fifteen days a few million words were hurled at the receptive conferees, almost beyond capability of absorption. Thus, we arrive at one of the great values of such joint, coordinated thinking and activity: to serve as a guide to the development of Christendom during the next five to seven years before another Assembly. We sense the direction of the travel and behind the push of man's progress we feel the pull of God's redemptive purpose which he purposed in Christ Jesus.

## Collaboration with the Roman Catholic Church

The great Commissions of the Council may meet yearly to consolidate individual and group research and development, such as the Commission on Faith and Order to which the Council elected nine Roman Catholic members for the first time. A three-year-old joint working group was approved by the Council to continue collaborating with the Roman Catholic Church. A permanent joint Roman Catholic-World Council of Churches Committee on society, development and peace was also set up to continue through these next years. Great

spiritual joy was expressed at the fraternal and cordial relationships continuing to develop between the Roman Catholic Church and the churches of the World Council, made possible by the forward spiritual guidance of Vatican II and the changing climate of possibilities since then.

## No Superchurch

To say all this, is to restate that the World Council of Churches is no Superchurch. It is a loosely knit working relationship of all churches committed to "unity in Christ," as simple as that. It makes no demands to any church to give up any of its beliefs or practices. It hopes that by bringing together the churches in ecumenicity that the love of God will permeate the more rapid development of Christendom for his mission on earth.

## The Need for Renewal

Who of us meeting at Uppsala did not feel earnestly that "God makes new" through the demands of "the worship, discipline and mutual correction of a world-wide community . . . that the ecumenical movement must become bolder, more representative . . . that our churches must acknowledge that this movement binds us to renewal."

This is the "new humanity in Christ" through which we find meaning, unity, and relevance to the needs of this world. This is the voice of God speaking to the churches today above the din of the world's wild war music, the

*(continued on page 56)*

# Jericho Road Philosophies

## By Carl W. McGeehon

EACH of us has a philosophy of life. Most of us are not articulate enough to write down in detail what we believe or to set forth clearly the principles which govern our conduct. It is possible to see in the actions of others, however, certain basic attitudes toward life which we may or may not share.

The familiar story of the good Samaritan (Luke 10:25-37) suggests four philosophies which are very much alive in our world today. The characters in this parable represent attitudes which each of us is tempted to adopt at one time or another. This story is a sort of a mirror in which we can see ourselves.

### Mine to Take

First we have the philosophy of the bandits. These villains pounced upon a lonely traveler on the road to Jericho, beat him, robbed him, and left him wounded by the side of the road.

The bandits' attitude toward life was "might makes right." If they had been articulate they might have phrased their philosophy of life in these words: *What is yours is mine if I can take it*. This is a very old principle of conduct. We think of Genghis Khan in the Orient, Alexander in the Near East, Napoleon in Europe, the warlords in China, the Maharajas in India, the unscrupulous robber-barons and monopolies in our own history, and the totalitarian governments of more recent times. In their lust for power men have ridden ruthlessly and roughshod over the rights of their fellowmen.

This philosophy of exploitation is by no means confined to those who have unlimited power or who carry a gun and wear a mask. In its more refined form we find it exemplified in everyday life.

A few years ago a team of investigators from *Reader's Digest* conducted an experiment to test the honesty of garage mechanics.

*Chaplain McGeehon is retired from the Air Force, serving as professor of Sociology, Texas Woman's University, Denton, Tex.*

They would stop their mechanically-perfect automobile a short distance from a garage and disconnect a wire which would slightly impair the performance of the car. Then they would drive to the garage and ask to have someone look at their motor. The adjustment could be made in a moment and many mechanics quickly replaced the wire and refused payment. A disturbingly high percentage, however, wanted to replace every conceivable part and charge every conceivable price to repair the car. Garagemen are neither better nor worse than average Americans. This experiment merely points up how widespread this philosophy of exploitation is in our society.

To take advantage of ignorance or weakness, to misuse power or rank or authority is to take the position of the Jericho road bandits. To trample on the rights of others on a small scale differs from the ruthlessness of tyrants only in degree, not kind.

The philosophy "what is yours is mine if I can take it," eats at the heart of our moral civilization. If there is any right or wrong in this universe, that way of living and that attitude toward life must surely bring upon itself suffering and ultimate defeat, whether practiced on an international scale or in an individual life.

## Mine to Keep

A second philosophy is represented by the priest and Levite. As Jesus told the story these two men passed by the unfortunate victim on the other side of the road. They may have been good, moral, law-abiding citizens but they felt no sense of responsibility for aiding a fellowman in trouble. Theirs was the sin of indifference.

Their unconcern for a man in need might be expressed in these words: *What is mine is mine and I intend to keep it for myself.* They believed in minding their own business but they were guilty of a neglect and indifference which bordered on callousness.

We see this attitude expressed in word and deed every day. Good people who would never think of hurting anyone will not take responsibility in helping those who have been hurt by others or by circumstances beyond their control. How different this is from Paul's injunction: "As we have opportunity, let us do good to all men." Or as James reminds us: "Whoever knows what is right to do and fails to do it, for him it is sin."

There is insight in the story of the hunter who had what he thought was an animal in his gunsight. He held his fire for a moment and it turned out the animal was a man. As he lowered his gun the man came close enough that the hunter recognized him as his own brother.

Spiritually, as well as physically, the world is round and sooner or later a man has to face up and take responsibility for his attitudes and actions. A philosophy of indifference, a reluctance to take responsibility for helping a brother in need is not an adequate basis upon which to build a life or a society. A Christian does not live to or for himself alone.

## Mine to Trade

The third character in this story who had a philosophy we see at work in the world was the innkeeper. It was to his place of business that the good Samaritan brought the wounded victim. He was no doubt a moral, upright man. There is no hint of anything shady or unscrupulous about him. But he represents a type of mind which acts on the principle: *What is mine is yours if you pay me for it.* This suggests the golden rule in reverse: not "I'll treat you as I hope you will treat me," but rather "as you treat me, so will I treat you." Jesus does not condemn the innkeeper, but neither is he the hero of this story.

The implication here is that the innkeeper was completely business-like and materialistic. He was a realist. He would not take unfair advantage of anyone but neither would he give more than he bargained for. He had a keen sense of justice but no understanding of mercy.

## Mine to Share

The man whom Jesus commended is the one we know as the good Samaritan. As he traveled toward Jericho he came upon a man who was bruised, beaten, and wounded. He stopped and ministered to him. Not only that, he put the victim upon his own beast, took him to an inn, and insured his comfort for the remainder of his recovery.

The Samaritan was in no way responsible for the traveler's misfortune. He did not know him. There was little likelihood he would ever see him again. Moreover, the wounded man was of a different race — one that despised the Samaritans heartily. But there was a goodness, a concern, a spirit of human brotherhood in the Samaritan's heart that could not let human suffering and need go unattended. His was a philosophy of love. He gave of his means and he gave of himself.

*What is mine is yours if you need it.* This is the attitude toward life which Jesus commends. Of it he said, "Go, and do likewise." The only life that counts, the only life that can bring satisfaction in the living, the only life that can fulfill God's purpose here on earth is the one built on the principle, "What is mine is yours if you need it."

In the world about us we see these four philosophies of the Jericho Road at work in the lives of people. Which of these reflects our basic philosophy of life? Mine to take, mine to keep, mine to trade, or mine to share? Only the philosophy of the Samaritan has love, good will, and sense of responsibility adequate to build a meaningful life or an enduring civilization. The way of love reflects the mind of Christ. ■■

In Texas a native who expresses a desire to go to heaven, is considered a traitor.—Jack Herbert.

# Achievement: Crown of Masculinity

### By Clifford Stevens

THE HUMAN MALE has a passion for achievement. This is the crown of his manhood and the goal of his efforts in every sphere of human affairs. This is true whether he be a boy flying a kite or a president leading a nation; whether he be Airman or General, Indian or Chief. He must see the imprint of his labor and his genius upon something tangible or his self-esteem and his sense of his own worth diminishes and he becomes something less than a man.

To be aware of this, for one who commands, whatever be the level of his authority, is to possess an insight into the deepest workings of human nature, an insight which can make a man a genius as a leader of other men. For no man rules by authority alone; he rules other men at that point and in the particular manner that his authority and his personality touches their lives and draws from them the best that is in them. For a man to rule other men surely and effectively, it is necessary that his authority draw from them the best efforts and the deepest energies locked inside them.

Achievement is the child of man's labor; by it he puts the mark of his individuality upon his environment, by it he acquires a sense of his own identity and a measure of his own worth. To deny him this, is to choke him in the intimate recesses of his own being and to stifle in him the very breath by which he lives.

In a military society, where authority is the strong base from which all effort and labor proceed, there is great danger that, from the necessities and pressures of the moment, men will become something less than men because genuine achievement and forceful, personal labor are denied them. When this happens high morale is impossible and a creeping sense of inadequacy strips even the strongest man of a proper sense of his own worth.

THIS IS certainly the key to effective leadership in the military society where success is often dependent solely upon the judgment and action of one man. If he who commands tries only to impress his image upon those subject to him and to use them as the elements of his own personal achievement, he will succeed only in drawing from them the minimal effort and the most mediocre results. He will see himself reflected in their efforts and from this false measure of his own worth he can lose confidence in his own ability to command and thereby endanger his own effectiveness and the effectiveness of his whole command. This explains perhaps the trembling insecurity of many who command and the petty policies caricatured so well by the character of Captain Queeg in Herman Wouk's *The Caine Mutiny*. No man can build upon the ruins of another man's personal dignity, and to lead other men is quite different from leading a flock of geese or a procession of children.

To be masculine is to achieve, to create, and it is from the elements of his own being that a man achieves and creates. This is true whether a man is a military man or a poet, a foot-soldier or a physician, an air policeman or a movie actor. The military environment does not change the nature of masculinity and when the military environment forces a man into uncreative and unproductive roles, he finds masculine achievement on unwholesome levels dangerous to his moral, marital and mental well-being thereby creating for the military authority problems which could have been avoided somewhat by a more careful appraisal of its policies.

That "man does not live by bread alone" is not only a deep spiritual insight, it is the very law of man's being. He lives from a sense of his own worth, from the signposts of his own personal achievement, and he dies when a sense of his own value has been bled from him. A man's glory is in his children, and this not only in the physical sense. His labor, his art, his achievement bear the stamp of his originality and only in the measure and in the degree that he is permitted to achieve does he find fulfillment as a man and sink his roots into a security that is life-giving and filled with contentment. To help a man fulfill this deepest law of his being is the greatest task of leadership in the military whether he commands a handful of airmen or the crew of a B-52 on a combat mission.          ■ ■

\* \* \*

**The Macmillan Bible Atlas** by Yohanan Aharoni and Michael Avi-Yonah. The Macmillan Co., 866 Third Ave., New York, N. Y. 10022. $14.95.

262 color maps with integrated text depicting religious, political, military and economic events of the Old Testament, the interbiblical, New Testament, and early church periods in biblical history.

31

# Man Without a Road Map

### By W. J. Smart

WHEN WESTERN explorers cast off their moorings to sail into unchartered seas and map unknown regions of the world, they felt there never had been such a thrilling time before and that such a time would never come again. They rounded the Cape of Good Hope in 1489, they discovered the West Indies in 1492, they found a sea route to India in 1498, they mapped Brazil in 1500, and in 1513 they discovered a new sea of enormous magnitude, namely, the Pacific Ocean.

But no voyage or journey ever undertaken was frought with greater significance for the subsequent life of man than that of Abraham who, at the call of God, went out not knowing whither he went, a man without a road map, moving along a route he had never seen before, with nothing to guide him or beckon him save the inner compulsion of the Voice of God.

The boyhood of Abraham was exciting and colorful. He lived in Ur of the Chaldees, one of the gayest and wealthiest cities in the world, situated on the banks of the river Euphrates. Every day he stood enthralled on the banks of that river, watching ships arriving and departing from Ur, manned by romantic sailors, carrying bright-robed merchants who brought costly merchandise from far-off lands.

*The Reverend W. J. Smart D.D. is vicar of Sulgrave and rector of Thorpe Mandeville, N. Banbury, Oxon, England*

32

But Ur was a corrupt city, dominated by a sensuous worship, and given over to materialism. Abraham's father, Terah, recoiling from the luxury and profligacy about him, decided to leave Ur and start life afresh in some other place. Taking his entire family and all their dependents, he set out, although we have no idea where he envisaged to settle ultimately. Nor did Terah know. His soul was in rebellion against the sins of Ur, and he longed for a healthier and cleaner life for his children. He traveled as far as Haran — a long journey in those days — and there he died.

How much Abraham owed to the example and idealism of his father is uncertain, but traditions, not included in our scriptures, suggest that it was at the grave of his father that Abraham heard God's call to take up his father's unfinished journey and fulfill his father's unrealized ambition.

"The Lord had said unto Abraham, Get thee out ... unto a land that I will show thee" (Genesis 12:1 KJV). Many centuries later, the writer of Hebrews said of him, "And he went out, not knowing whither he went" (Hebrews 11:8 KJV).

At this time, Abraham was probably a shepherd chieftain of very little significance or importance in the eyes of his own generation. Does it not strike us as being a very extraordinary thing that such a man should be given the vision of founding a new kind of civilization? That he should envisage his posterity being as numerous as the stars of heaven and like the sand for multitude? Yet such was the vision of Abraham. He also believed that this great nation of the future would be held together by their peculiar faith in God, and that the purpose of their existence would be to channel God's blessing to the entire world.

"I will make of thee a great nation, and I will bless thee and make thy name great; and thou shalt be a blessing ... and in thee shall all the families of the earth be blessed" (Genesis 12:2, 3 KJV).

THROUGHOUT the Bible a great deal is said about Abraham's faith. It refers not only to his obedience but to his implicit trust in the promises of God; for he believed whatever God promised, although he knew it would be quite impossible for anyone to bring those promises to pass except God. Thus, God promised that he would be the founder of a great nation when, to begin with, he had no son and his wife was past childbearing. Then when the miracle happened, and Isaac had grown to youth, Abraham believed that God was calling him to sacrifice that very son in whom all his hopes for the future were centered.

Every life has its crucial test of character and faith, and it is always connected in some way with something we most love and value. There was nothing Abraham treasured so much as his son Isaac. Yet it seemed to Abraham that God was saying to him,

> Take now thy son, thine only son Isaac, whom thou lovest and get thee into the land of Moriah; and offer him there for a burnt offering upon one of the mountains which I will tell thee of. And Abraham rose up early in the morning, . . . and took Isaac his son, and clave the wood for the burnt offering . . . and went unto the place of which God had told him. . . And Abraham built an altar there, and laid the wood in order, and bound Isaac his son, and laid him on the altar upon the wood (Genesis 22:2-3, 9b).

It is extremely difficult for us in this twentieth century to enter into the psychology of this part of Abraham's story. It is entirely foreign to our conception of God and the nature and significance of man's relationship with God. It is equally alien to our conceptions of personal freedom and the sacredness of human personality, especially those individuals within our own family circle. To understand this incident at all requires a serious and imaginative attempt to decipher a whole tapestry of ideas which belong to a bygone age. After all, there are those who date the birth of Abraham at 2161 B.C. and it would be surprising if, in the light of Christ and all he has made known to the world, we had not learned a lot of new things about God since then.

Human sacrifices were not uncommon four thousand years ago. Nor was it uncommon for a father to prove his devotion to God by sacrificing his most beloved son. According to the ideas of the time, a son was the legal property of his father, to be retained or disposed of as the father saw fit. The more a father loved his son, the greater was thought to be the virtue in sacrificing him to God, for such a sacrifice demonstrated beyond all argument how much he loved God.

BUT WE HAVE here something more than Abraham's readiness to make a human sacrifice to prove his devotion to God. We have also the self-abnegation of his son. Isaac at this time was a young man with plenty of youthful energy and spirit, while Abraham on the other hand was an old man whom Isaac could have easily overpowered had he wanted to do so. Why did Isaac not refuse to be bound? Why did he not resist being laid upon the altar? He could not have been blind to his father's intentions. Why did not Isaac resist and rebel and run away?

Can it be that the conversations between father and son about "the lamb for the burnt offering" had brought Isaac to accept his father's viewpoint? Had Isaac, too, come to feel under his father's influence that this was the way God wanted it? Can it be that both father and son had resolved to go right on in obedience to what they believed was the divine will, hoping against hope that God would intervene to make the sacrifice unnecessary? Abraham and Isaac talked much together on the way to the mountains of Moriah, and Isaac asked his father "we have the wood and the fire, but where is the lamb for a burnt offering?" Abraham replied "My son, God will provide himself a lamb for a burnt offering." And after this we are told "They went both of them together" (Genesis 22:8). Does this togetherness refer only to physical proximity, or does it also refer to a spiritual togetherness, a union of wills? Has Abraham told Isaac all that was in his heart, all that God has said to him, promised him, commanded him, and the mystery of this final requirement to sacrifice the very one in whom all the promises of God were concentrated? Has Isaac accepted his father's faith, although it means for him self-sacrifice? Have they both, the aged father and youthful son, solemnly and sorrowfully agreed to go on with what they believe to be God's mysterious plan, both submitting themselves to a bewildering situation of intense pain and suffering which neither of them could understand?

Man's extremity is always God's opportunity. "Abraham, Abraham," called a voice as Abraham stretched forth his hand to slay Isaac. "Lay not thine hand upon the lad, neither do thou anything unto him; for now I know that thou fearest God, seeing thou has not withheld thy son, thine only son from me" (Gen. 22:12 KJV). That which makes an acceptable sacrifice is not what we place upon the altar, although that has its importance and significance, but the inner spirit in which we offer it.

Right from the moment of his original call, Abraham exhibited a mental attitude of trust in God, an emotional attitude of reliance upon God and a volitional attitude of total obedience to God. These were the fundamental secrets of his life, the high road he traveled in the fulfillment of God's plan.

G OD has a plan for every life, and a purpose for every life to fulfill. Just as the minutest piece of mechanism in your wrist watch is important and has a work to do; as every player in an orchestra, whether great or small, has an indispensable part to play to effect a perfect performance of the symphony, so with God's plan and its fulfillment for the human race. Abraham became the man he did and his faith became the example of faith for all time, because he listened to God when he spoke to him, and tried to carry out God's instructions.

Abraham proved in his own experience over four thousand years ago that the God who calls is also the God who guides and sustains when he is trusted and obeyed. It is when we walk with the Lord that he sheds a glory on our way, and no good thing does he withhold from them that walk uprightly. God showed Abraham day after day the road he should take and made provisions for all his needs. God kept all his promises; indeed, that was the most thrilling part of all— God kept all his promises.

Although you have no road map, you will not get lost if the hand of the Lord is leading you. If your life is in the hands of God you need not fear the unknown land before you, the unmapped country which you have to explore. But, you say, can we be sure that God's hand is leading us? Sometimes, yes; sometimes, no. Sometimes the call of God is so clear that we know beyond all doubt that we are on the right track; but there are other times when there is no voice to tell us the road to take, when even prayer does not clarify the situation for us, when all we can do is to commit our way unto Him and go forward in accordance with all we know of him, trusting him to bring us where he wants us to be. ■ ■

*Folk Songs and Hymns with Guitar Accompaniment*
    At the suggestion of the Committee on Ministry to Armed Forces Personnel, the YMCA has published a small booklet of 104 pages containing familiar folk songs and hymns with guitar accompaniment. The book has been amazingly successful. Those who wish to order copies may do so by sending a donation of 50 cents per copy. Write to:

> Howard B. Wilson, Director, Program and Publication Relations,
> National Council of the YMCAs of the USA,
> 291 Broadway, New York, N. Y.

# The Good Doctor and Basketball

WHY don't you have a good drinking spree instead of reading the Bible all of the time? You're nothing but a sissy!" With these harsh words spoken, the man was promptly flattened with one blow by the so-called "sissy." The man referred to by the rowdy was none other than Dr. James Naismith, the inventor of basketball.

James was an extraordinary athlete. His intention was to become a preacher and combine religion with sports. He entered McGill University at Montreal to prepare for his chosen vocation. At graduation time he was given the highest awards for all-around gym work at the University. Later he became the college's physical education director. After McGill, he attended and graduated from the Presbyterian Theological College in Montreal.

Naismith decided to enroll in the YMCA in Springfield, Massachusetts, with the idea of teaching clean living through sports. It was a good idea and proved to be 100 percent correct. It was while at the "Y" that one of the greatest games in sports was invented. How it came about was quite amusing.

There were 18 gentlemen enrolled at the school who cared little for sports and less for any kind of exercise. The task of involving these men in some kind of physical exercise was given to James with a two-week limit. Not one to walk away from a challenge, Naismith accepted. His plan was to invent a new game to draw their interest. He studied the problem for a time and hit upon an idea. Summoning his building custodian, he asked him for several small wooden boxes. The custodian promptly returned with several peach baskets. James then mounted the baskets on a wooden pole ten feet above the floor — one at each end of the gym. He divided the reluctant class into two teams of nine men each.

At first the men showed no inclination of tossing the ball into the baskets, but after a few tosses they played with enthusiasm. From that day on basketball has grown into one of the fastest and most popular sports in the world ... through the teachings of a minister who believed in the Bible and clean living.

—**Mario DeMarco**

37

# He Sought the Secrets of the Pole

## By Charles Ludwig

Captain Robert Scott, who led the expedition to the South Pole, was a man of dreams and courage.

AS THE fierce Antarctic winds howled about his tent, Captain Robert Falcon Scott knew that he and his three companions would soon freeze to death. The last bite of food had been swallowed, and although there was a large supply of pemmican and other edibles in a food depot a mere eleven miles away, he knew it would be impossible to get to it.

Fearing that Scott and his men might come to just such an end as this, those who had prepared this 1910 expedition to the South Pole, had sent along a supply of opium.

A dose of this would send the trapped men into a land of pleasant dreams and they would not fear the terrors of the cold. Death was now rattling the frozen flaps of their tent; but instead of reaching for the opium, Scott fumbled for his pen and paper in order to address letters he hoped would reach his wife and

**The tragic but gallant story of Robert Scott and his men who arrived at the South Pole one month too late**

small son, Peter, and his friends.

During those last tragic hours, Scott and his companions felt the strength that comes to those who trust in "the everlasting arms." The evidence of this is shown in the letters found eight months later in notebooks wedged beneath Scott's shoulders.

Today, Captain Robert Falcon Scott has become a symbol of courage to the world, and the diaries of his last expedition are being read again and again.

THE Antarctica, "a giant refrigerator with a leak," has fascinated men ever since its mainland was discovered by Captain Nathaniel Brown Palmer, an American searching for seals in 1820. Since then, in spite of winds that frequently blow at 200 miles an hour; and of temperatures that sag to 125 degrees below zero, the nations of the world have sought to explore its treasures.

From the time Scott became a naval cadet at the age of thirteen, he dreamed of visiting Antarctica. And sometimes when his daydreams got wild, he imagined being the first one to reach the South Pole. As his father watched him during this period, he shook his head and called him "old mooney." But Scott tied his dreams to real work. He passed the rather stiff examinations during his twentieth year with honors and was made a sub-lieutenant.

He could have been content with his position in the British Navy. It had security and offered steady advancement; but his vision and energy would not allow this. He dug into every book he could find to learn about the areas beyond the Antarctica Circle. He was grimly determined that some day he was going to sail into and explore that mysterious land.

This interest came to the attention of others. When he was only thirty-one he was chosen to lead the first British Expedition to explore the practically unknown Antarctic Continent — a continent two-thirds as large as North America. Sailing from England in 1900, he led the party to the land of his dreams.

Scott's ship, *Discovery*, returned to England on September 10, 1904. Scott was given a hero's welcome and was promoted to Captain. These honors were deserved, for he and his party, in spite of great difficulty, had explored the Victoria Mountains; the Ross Ice Barrier; and had discovered and named King Edward Island.

ENTHUSIASM for the ice-capped land to the south that surrounded the bottom of the world like a saucer continued to spread throughout the world, and that enthusiasm overpowered Scott. In 1909 he announced that he was organizing a second expedition, and on June 1, 1910, he sailed the *Terra*

*Nova* down the Thames on the first part of his journey to the Pole.

Scott knew the courageous Norwegian, Roald Amundsen, was also leading an expedition of discovery. But since Amundsen was supposed to be heading for the *North* Pole; he felt he would have no difficulty in being the first man to reach the *South* Pole, and proudly to plant a fluttering Union Jack on that unclaimed spot.

With great confidence, Scott sailed toward McMurdo Sound where he intended to establish a base and a string of supply depots stretching toward the Pole. These food depots were necessary to provide the necessities of life on the way from the Pole—should they reach it.

The men were optimistic—perhaps too optimistic. On Christmas Day they crowded the room on the ship where the services were held, listened to the reading of the Word and sang hymns honoring the birth of Christ. One of the men's rabbits gave birth to 17 little ones that day, and so optimistic was the owner he gave away 22 of them!

The *Terra Nova* was duly anchored at McMurdo Sound on January 3, 1911. And then the work of building a solid base was commenced. Scott wrote in his diary with enthusiasm about the men. *"Thursday, January 5.* All hands were up at 5 this morning. Words cannot express the splendid way in which everyone works and gradually the work gets organized. I was a little late on the scene this morning, and thereby witnessed a most extra-

ordinary scene. Some 6 to 7 killer whales, old and young, were skirting the fast floe ahead of the ship...."

Scott had hoped the weather and other items of chance would work in his favor; but now that his base was established, and his depots placed in order, everything seemed to go wrong. Everything! Although advised to rely on dogs, Scott felt that ponies were the answer—that they could pull the sleds over longer distances before tiring. And, in order that his ponies might be prepared for the cold, he had had them hardened in the cold steppes of Siberia.

Alas, this decision was a major mistake. The ponies, terrified with the snow and ice, stampeded and broke their legs in the many crevasses and had to be shot. And what dogs they had, big huskies from the Yukon, failed to perform as expected. Some went wild. Others fell into the deep cracks that crossed the glaciers.

And then word came that Amundsen had established a base at the Bay of Whales. This meant the Norwegian was headed for the South Pole! It was a stinging blow. But Scott merely winced for a moment. With courage, he wrote: "One thing only fixes itself definitely in my mind.... To go forward and do our best for the honor of the country without fear or panic."

The race was on!

WITHOUT animals to help them, Scott and four of his men harnessed themselves to a thousand-pound sled and headed

Scott's party included Wilson, Oates, Bowers, and Evans. They reached the South Pole, but died on the way back. Bowers, seated on the left, pulled the string for this historical picture. Scott stands in the center. His diary found eight months later told how the men suffered to reach their goal and died a few miles from their depot.

for the South Pole—the final objective of all their dreams. The going was rough. Blizzards, from the vast white silence whistled down on them, lashing and cutting their faces. Pulling the sled in the thin, more than 10,000 feet high atmosphere at the bottom of the world, drained what small energy they had left after a year and a-half of struggle, pain, and homesickness. But the hope of being the first to the Pole drove them on like a scourge. Knowing the value of his diaries, Scott continued to keep notes on their progress.

*"Thursday, January 11.* Height 10,530. Temp. —25.8°. About 74 miles from the Pole—can we keep this up for seven days? It takes it out of us like anything. None of us ever had such hard work before."

Five days later, keen disappointment faced the little group. But although a near-despair gripped him, Scott bravely jotted down the facts.

*"Tuesday, January 16.* Camp 68. Height 9,760. T. —23.5°. The worst has happened, or nearly the worst. ...Bower's sharp eyes detected what he thought was a cairn (a heap of stones).... Soon we knew it could be no natural snow feature. We marched on, found that it was a black flag tied to a sledge bearer.

Scott, Bowers, and Wilson died in a severe storm only eleven miles from supplies. This wooden cross stands where the bodies of Scott, Bowers, and Wilson were found by another party eight months after their deaths. The bodies of Oates and Evans were never found.

...All the daydreams must go...."
Still there was hope, a chance in a million that by some curious fate they could still be first to get to that most difficult spot. Scott filled his lungs with the rare, frigid air, gripped the Union Jack and prayed. He forced his bone-weary feet to go on and strained his eyes. Then he and his companions saw what they

42

had hoped they would never see. Choking back his emotions, Scott jotted it down.

*"Thursday morning, January 18.* Decided after summing up all observations that we are 3.5 miles away from the Pole. . . . Bowers saw a cairn or tent. . . . In the tent we find a record of five Norwegians having been here. . . ."

Amundsen had beaten them to the Pole! There could be no doubt about it, now. Scott left a note in the tent, indicating that he had visited it. Then he went on ahead to what he considered the very center of the Pole and fastened the Union Jack to a "piece of stick."

Using dog teams, the Norwegians had reached the South Pole on December 16, 1911. Scott, arriving on January 17, 1912, had been beaten nearly a month!

Scott's last sentence in his diary on that day of searing disappointment is a masterpiece of courageous acceptance. "Well, we have turned our back now on the goal of our ambition and must face our 800 miles of solid dragging — and goodby to most of the daydreams."

THE WAY back was filled with heartbreaking disaster. Evans — perhaps the strongest man physically in the group — slipped on the ice, crushed his skull and died. Oates' feet were so frostbitten he could barely keep up. Knowing that he was hindering the others, he calmly announced, "I am going outside. I may be gone for some time." He never returned, and his body has never been found.

Staggering, stumbling, hoping, praying, Scott and the two survivors kept going. Their faces and feet froze and became brittle. The miles before them stretched out, and out. . . . The white silences of snow and ice sneered and mocked them. But they continued on, hoping for an impossible break. If only the weather would change. . . .

Then, eleven miles from fuel and food, an unusual blizzard began to blow. The blizzard meant that all hope was gone. The men pitched a tent, and while the fury of the storm tore at them, they continued to talk and plan and pray.

Scott's last entry in his notebook was on Thursday, March 29. "Since the 21st we have had a continuous gale. . . . We had fuel to make two cups of tea apiece and bare food for two days on the 20th. Every day we have been ready to start for our depot eleven miles away, but outside the door of the tent it remains a scene of whirling drift. . . . We shall stick it out to the end, but we are getting weaker, of course, and the end cannot be far.

"It seems a pity, but I do not think I can write more."

Then, thinking of his family, he added a postscript.

"For God's sake look after our people."

Eight months later, those who found the bodies along with the diaries, buried the men under a cross of two skiis lashed together.

Over the grave, they wrote some words from Tennyson which included this line:

*(continued on page 56)*

# Waiting for Joye

## By Anne Langworthy

### Nothing is more lonely than a New Year's Eve alone

IT'S New Year's Eve and here I am sitting alone by the TV all because of my sister. Perhaps I'm a dope not to hate her, but I don't. All I want is a chance to do things my way. But somehow I always end up doing things her way.

Like tonight. I could have been at a swinging party back home with Doug, my steadiest boy friend. But Joye wanted to come back today because she had a big party. She's twenty and in her third year; I'm eighteen and in my first semester.

Doug didn't like it, of course. He hadn't liked it when I came to the University instead of going to State with him. But Joye was already here and we could share an apartment. That's a laugh! Look around and all you see is Joye's things. And Joye could look after me, The Parents said. They voted for it, so that was that! Three to

one. And we're a family that believes in democracy and all that jazz.

My parents are great. Really, I mean. Average American middle class. Salt of the earth. Dad and Mom married after he got out the Navy. World War II. They didn't have much except youth and love and they've worked hard. All the way from two furnished rooms to a brick rambler in Lake Bluff and two daughters at TU. They never told me, but Nana did. She's pretty partial to Dad—her baby—and she told me Dad gave up the country club to send us to college. Nana doesn't believe much in what she calls the modern trend of young people running their parents.

Mom's a good sport, too! Bruz and Sis are in elementary yet, but she works part-time—running around like crazy every day. I mean, The Parents are rather young

and should be enjoying life, I suppose.

I thought I was included in Joye's party. I never had been before. But I know Joye's friends. How could I help it? They're sprawled all over our living room every night. But Joye told Dad I could go 'cause he knew about the party at home and the date with Doug. Driving back she even said I could wear her pink chiffon and we planned what I'd wear with it...

But that was before she got the phone call—right after we got back. I knew it was from Brad when I answered. I went on unpacking. She came in looking like she was going to cry. When I saw that, my heart thudded straight to my toes. And it's still there. I knew what to expect before she said, "We're a man short. Brad's trying..." Trying hard, I thought. I didn't like Brad. Joye never seemed to play favorites, but I hoped that Brad wouldn't end up my brother-in-law.

Well, what could I do? I wondered if other girls—and boys, too—ever had problems like mine. But I mumbled, "Don't worry. I've got three exams and I need to study..."

"I promised Dad..." She knew I'd never tell. After all I'd given up the party with my friends—and Doug, who I wouldn't see again 'til spring break. And I probably wouldn't like it with her friends, anyway. Joye had told The Parents about it. Twelve couples. Dinner at the River Boat, and then to Brad's Pad. I'd never seen it, but Joye described it. Penthouse atop a glass tower on the river. Fur rugs. Wide black leather couches. Stone fireplace that worked. Solid walls of real paintings. A balcony even. Real cool. Doesn't that sound like a student apartment?

Actually, Brad and Rich shared it. Brad was the rich one—son of an oil millionaire. Rich's father was a senator. Both Rich and Brad are political science majors and going into politics. Joye picked them up in American history. She picks up men as if she were Liz Taylor, or something.

You really have to see Joye to know what I mean. She's beautiful. She sort of looks at a man from her blue eyes under those thick black lashes—real, too—and wham!— they'd follow her anywhere. It's been that way as long as I can remember. Joye was The Parent's first child, and the grandparents first grandchild. After the war, too, when they'd worried about Dad. Well, they made her real special. I came along sort of unexpectedly two years later with two other grandchildren. I was scrawny, dark-haired, red, spitting, crying. And Joye had just arrived at the adorable stage. You know what The Parents named me? Theodora! For the grandmothers. I wondered how they could do that to me. But it wouldn't have made any difference if I'd been Joye, and she'd been

Theodora. It's just like she's got a magnet inside her that links up with a magnet inside other people. Not just men, either. The Parents— little old ladies and little old men. Bruz. Sis. And even me.

BRAD picked her up at eight. She looked like an angel—a blue one, all soft-draped chiffon and glimmering rhinestones. Her smile sparkled like a million of them all together. Brad had a blue-throated white orchid that matched as if it'd been grown just for her.

"'Bye, Ted. Don't wait up."

"Happy New Year," I said. They didn't need my good wishes; they really had happiness. I turned off TV and finished unpacking. I put on my new brown Christmas slacks with my new turtleneck sweater, brown and beige stripes. I looked in the mirror and thought I looked pretty good with my chestnut wavy hair and my golden brown eyes. But no sparkle.

I tried to settle down on the sofa with my books. It was too quiet so I turned television on again. They were playing old songs that sort of lumped my throat, so I twisted the switch savagely. I got out a Coke, and remembered I hadn't had any dinner. Maybe I'd feel better if I ate, but I didn't feel like it.

Darn! All semester I'd cooked, washed dishes, scrubbed floors . . . and what good did it do? I mean, who cared? Joye's friends sprawled around eating the cookies I baked, and drinking milk by the gallon, which I lugged home. Joye told me I should send them home, but I

46

wasn't the one who made two or three dates every night and was always late for them.

At first it embarrassed me — then it exasperated me when I had to study. Eventually, I went about my business — cleaning, cooking, studying, rolling up my hair even. At ten I put them out on the welcome mat, the fellows I mean. It never embarrassed Joye. And the fellows didn't mind. One smile from her blue eyes and they would have waited two more hours. They'd wait, so she let them. I hoped that just once one of them would walk out on her. But none of them ever

did. Well, I couldn't care less. I was here to get an education, and then marry Doug.

Until I met Rich, that is. One night I let him in because Joye was still in the shower.

"Hi, little sister!"

"Hi, Senator!" I'd heard about him, too.

He had laughed merrily. I looked up and his laughing dark eyes met mine, and it affected me just like Joye's blue eyes got to all the guys. What I mean, I would have walked out of that apartment and followed him anywhere. He'd never have any trouble getting elected so long as there were women who voted.

Well, he was around a lot after that. Joye let him wait, too. But we got along fine. I fed him cookies, milk, pizza, homemade fudge. And he talked politics. I knew all about his family, his father's career. I just sat there listening and dreaming.

I TURNED on the TV and the New Year was being welcomed at Times Square. The clock chimed eleven. Well, I was trying to write a theme for my English class. New Year's Eve. I thought about Joye and the gang at the River House. And I thought about Doug with the old crowd. I stood looking at jammed Times Square, and I had never felt so lonely in my life. And then there was a knock on the door. My heart skipped, then raced. Rich's rat-a-tat-tat! I leaped to the door. My heart leaped to my throat. I opened the door. And there he stood!

"Hi, little sister. Where's Joye?" He looked elegant in one of those new tuxes with turtleneck and Nehru jacket.

"Not here."

"Where is she?"

"With Brad."

"I just came from the Pad. No one there."

"She left at eight. Maybe they're still at the River House."

He grabbed the phone and called. He turned away, frowning. "They left there an hour ago."

"Maybe they're back now."

He dialed his number and let it ring seven times. I counted. "No one there." He hung up.

48

"Well," I picked up the papers scattered across the floor, "you might as well wait there as here. Joye won't be back." I felt angry, maybe even jealous for Joye having two dates on New Year's Eve and having conned me out of one.

"Are you sure?"

"I'm sure."

He looked at me thoughtfully. "I told her The Senator was coming for the Governor's reception tomorrow. My car broke down so I was late, but I called Brad..."

"Brad? He knew?"

"I told him to have Joye wait. I was coming as fast as I could. The folks are giving a party at the Rose Room..."

The Rose Room of the Park-Hilton. I'd never been there, either. "He didn't tell her."

"You sure?"

"Why don't you find her and ask?" I turned away.

He looked at his watch. "I haven't time." He looked at me. "What are you doing?"

"What does it look like? Spending a quiet evening at home writing about my deliriously happy New Year's Eve."

"Stood up?"

"No."

He kept on looking at me and I saw the idea beginning to form in his mind. "Oh, no. I've substituted for Joye since I was born. And I've babysat her friends all semester. But that's that. I've made a New Year's resolution..."

He smiled. "I think you're right. You've understudied for Joye long enough. Now a midnight supper at the Rose Room with The Senator might bore Joye..." He was a little put out, and I couldn't blame him.

I remembered I was very hungry. And meeting The Senator! A warm feeling sort of bubbled up from my toes and put a sparkle in my eyes.

"You'll have to hurry."

"You mean you'd take me?" It didn't sound as casual as I'd like.

"Grab your coat."

"And I wouldn't be just a substitute for Joye?"

He cupped my elbows lightly with his hands, and shook his head. "No. Get ready." He gave me a little push toward the bedroom.

I turned at the door and said, "The only dress I've got is one of Joye's."

"Well, wear her dress, but be yourself." He picked up a box he'd dropped on the table and tossed it to me.

I opened it. It was a corsage of violets and sweetheart roses. I gasped. "They're lovely!" I put them against my cheek.

"You've got just fifteen minutes."

Fourteen and one-half minutes later by the clock I came out wearing the pale pink chiffon.

"Wow!" he said, and his eyes had golden lights in them. "Wow! Do you know, Teddy, that I've never seen you dressed up before?"

"You've got to be kidding!"

He pinned the corsage on, rather expertly I noted. Then he put his fingers under my chin, kissed me lightly on the cheek.

"Happy New Year, Teddy."

I felt like laughing, shouting, singing Hallelujah, crying, and throwing myself in his arms. But I merely lowered my lashes demurely and said, "And a happy New Year to you, too, Rich." ■ ■

# Daily Bible Readings

## January

| DAY | BOOK | CHAPTER |
|---|---|---|
| 1 | Hebrews | 11:1-12 |
| 2 | Genesis | 11:31-12:9 |
| 3 | Genesis | 12:10-20 |
| 4 | Genesis | 13:1-11 |
| 5 | Genesis | 13:12-18 |
| 6 | Genesis | 14:1-16 |
| 7 | Genesis | 14:17-24 |
| 8 | Genesis | 15:1-6 |
| 9 | Genesis | 15:7-21 |
| 10 | Genesis | 16:1-14 |
| 11 | Genesis | 16:15-17:8 |
| 12 | Genesis | 17:9-14 |
| 13 | Genesis | 17:15-21 |
| 14 | Genesis | 17:22-27 |
| 15 | Genesis | 18:1-15 |
| 16 | Genesis | 18:16-21 |
| 17 | Genesis | 18:22-33 |
| 18 | Genesis | 19:1-11 |
| 19 | Genesis | 19:12-23 |
| 20 | Genesis | 19:24-30 |
| 21 | Genesis | 21:1-14 |
| 22 | Genesis | 21:15-21 |
| 23 | Genesis | 22:1-14 |
| 24 | Genesis | 22:15-19 |
| 25 | Genesis | 23:1-16 |
| 26 | Genesis | 24:1-9 |
| 27 | Genesis | 24:10-27 |
| 28 | Genesis | 24:28-51 |
| 29 | Genesis | 24:52-25:8 |
| 30 | Romans | 4:1-25 |
| 31 | Acts | 7:2-8 |

# God Enough and

# Enough God for Me

## By Frederick Ward Kates

SPEAKING against the background of the agonizing difficulty hosts of people are experiencing these days regarding belief in God, in his knowability, even in his reality and existence, I wish to declare, directly and forthrightly, that Jesus Christ is God enough and enough God for me. This declaration is nothing other than the statement any man can and may and does make who has found and encountered the living God in Jesus Christ, who has found the avenue to God through Jesus Christ, who has discovered in Jesus Christ the truth about God, and who in union with Jesus Christ finds he shares in the very life of God. That, basically, is what causes that man to be styled a Christian—the fact that in Jesus Christ he finds God and that in him God shines through to him.

The Christian is as vividly cognizant of "the problem of God" as any man, and also the element of mystery in life. As acutely as any other man, he is aware of the difficulty of completely comprehending God, though steadily as he stands fast in discipleship he humbly believes he is growing in apprehension of God. He is as puzzled and baffled by the perplexing ways of life and of God as any man. The reverent and profound agnosticism of every intelligent and thinking man marks him as it characterizes every reflective and sensitive human being. God is as much a mystery to him, and God's ways and works, as to any other.

## God Hides Himself

As the Christian views the matter, the whole universe and pattern of human life indicate neither a total exclusion nor a manifest presence of Divinity but the presence of a

*Mr. Kates is rector of St. Paul's Church in Bergen, 38 Duncan Ave., Jersey City, N.J. 07304*

God who hides himself. It is the man of deepest faith who experiences what all the saints call "the dark night of the soul." One thinks of Job, afflicted with all manner of suffering, trying to reason with God whose ways he cannot understand. One thinks of that great collection of the voices of faith, the Psalter, and such cries addressed to God as "Why dost thou stand afar off, O Lord? Why dost thou hide thyself in times of trouble?" (Psalm 10:1). And one remembers Jesus on the Cross crying out in his agony another verse from the Psalms: "My God, my God, why hast thou forsaken me? Why art thou so far from helping me, from the words of my groaning?" (Psalm 22:1).

Yes, be well assured, the Christian knows ample about the God who hides, the God who is incomprehensible by our limited, human understanding, whose ways are not our ways and whose thoughts are not our thoughts. But the Christian differs from the strident voices of recent months and years sounding-off in sermon, lecture, book and interview that God is dead or never existed at all just because God does not now, as he has not in the past, chosen to disclose himself totally to his creatures' minds. Granted it is not easy to live on the terms that apparently we must live on, but the Christian does not fight the fact, rather he accepts it, and goes on his way rejoicing that he has as much light as he does have, for which he unceasingly thanks God.

God has not, does not, and in all likelihood will not, fully disclose himself to man, though angry men berate him for not doing so. It is idle and vain to look to God to trace across the sky in smoke-writing the words "I am not dead" or any such statement that might satisfy non-believers that he exists and is still God. God is a God who hides but he is also a God who furnishes us with hints and gives us clues as to his reality and presence.

## God Declares Himself

The most eloquent hint and the chief clue to knowledge of himself that the God who hides himself from men has given to the world, according to Christian conviction, is a person, a human being fashioned like unto ourselves, namely, he who was born a child to Mary, who was espoused to Joseph, the carpenter of Nazareth, in Bethlehem of Judea on a clear winter's night, as nearly as we can calculate, 1,961 years ago. In Jesus, Mary's child, God declared himself, came out of hiding, so to speak, and disclosed himself, his nature and purpose, in a unique way. In Jesus God is crucially focused and expressed in human life, Christians believe. "In Christ God became specific," to use Dr. Theodore P. Ferris' words. "Christ is the very embodiment of God in human life," according to theologian Roger Hazelton; and, in William Temple's words, "What we see as we watch the life of Jesus is the very life of heaven—indeed of God —in human expression."

The God men of today find so hard to know and to understand —this God has declared himself in

51

Jesus Christ, Christians believe. At a certain time and point in human history and in a specific human person—Jesus of Nazareth, God himself entered into human life, Christians affirm, thus giving men the knowledge they yearn for: certain and certified knowledge of God. In him God came out of hiding and revealed himself to men and for men definitively and decisively. Believing this is why Christians are called Christians.

To Christians and for them, Christ is light in darkness, for who believes in him no longer abides in darkness regarding the nature of God, or how to get to God. With joy and gratitude Christians welcome and accept Christ as God's supreme gift to men. In their actual experience they find him to be their means of access to God and God's avenue of address to them. In him they find true knowledge of and about God and in union with him they share the life of God.

### God Gives Himself

From what one hears in theological circles and reads these days, there are many men who want, and boldly demand, more of God than God has designed to give them. But have we not received enough of God in Jesus Christ and God enough in him for all our wants and needs? God's self-revelation in Christ is enough for a vast multitude of men and, for myself, speaking as one of this number, Jesus Christ is God enough for me—for my every desire and need, and in himself more than enough God to command my glad adoration and joyous praise. And I am humbly grateful that this is so, for we have no assurance at all that any further and fuller self-disclosure by God will be granted us. God came to this world once to die for it on a cross. When he comes again, he will come in majesty and power and as the world's Judge.

True—undeniably true, the world is a dark place in many aspects, and for men life remains, and probably will always remain, a puzzling experience. But—and this is Christianity's good news—you and I and every man have quite enough light to live by, and to live gloriously and thankfully, in God's supreme gift to us, namely, himself in his Son. In him and through him, we can and do know God. In him and through him, God has provided a way back home to himself, and as much truth and light as a man needs for his earthly pilgrimage. He is the living link between heaven and earth, and joining our lives with his we may share in God's own life, investing them with God's eternal life.

Thanks be to God for his unspeakable gift—Jesus Christ, who is God enough and enough God for me, and, I dare to hope, likewise for you; and who, we find, when we love him and seek to live our lives after his fashion, is, in fact, the way to God and God's way to us, the full measure of the truth about himself that God has granted men, and the actual life of God made available to us and accessible for us. ■■

52

# STATEMENT OF OWNERSHIP, MANAGEMENT AND CIRCULATION

*(Act of October 23, 1962; Section 4369, Title 39, United States Code)*

Publisher: File two copies of this form with your postmaster.
Postmaster: Complete verification on page 2

Form Approved, Budget Bureau No. 46–R029

| 1. DATE OF FILING | 2. TITLE OF PUBLICATION |
|---|---|
| 9/24/68 | THE LINK |

3. FREQUENCY OF ISSUE

Monthly

4. LOCATION OF KNOWN OFFICE OF PUBLICATION *(Street, city, county, state, ZIP code)*

1420 P Street, Lincoln, Nebraska  68501

5. LOCATION OF THE HEADQUARTERS OR GENERAL BUSINESS OFFICES OF THE PUBLISHERS *(Not printers)*

122 Maryland Ave., N. E., Washington, D. C. 20002

6. NAMES AND ADDRESSES OF PUBLISHER, EDITOR, AND MANAGING EDITOR

PUBLISHER *(Name and address)* The General Commission on Chaplains and Armed Forces Personnel
Exec.     122 Maryland Ave., N. E., Washington, D. C. 20002

EDITOR *(Name and address)* The Rev. A. Ray Appelquist,
122 Maryland Ave., N. E., Washington, D. C. 20002

MANAGING EDITOR *(Name and address)* The Rev. Lawrence P. Fitzgerald,
122 Maryland Ave., N. E., Washington, D. C. 20002

7. OWNER *(If owned by a corporation, its name and address must be stated and also immediately thereunder the names and addresses of stockholders owning or holding 1 percent or more of total amount of stock. If not owned by a corporation, the names and addresses of the individual owners must be given. If owned by a partnership or other unincorporated firm, its name and address, as well as that of each individual must be given.)*

| NAME | ADDRESS |
|---|---|
| The General Commission on Chaplains and Armed Forces Personnel | 122 Maryland Ave., N. E., Washington, D. C. 20002 |

8. KNOWN BONDHOLDERS, MORTGAGEES, AND OTHER SECURITY HOLDERS OWNING OR HOLDING 1 PERCENT OR MORE OF TOTAL AMOUNT OF BONDS, MORTGAGES OR OTHER SECURITIES *(If there are none, so state)*

| NAME | ADDRESS |
|---|---|
| None | |

9. FOR COMPLETION BY NONPROFIT ORGANIZATIONS AUTHORIZED TO MAIL AT SPECIAL RATES *(Section 132.122, Postal Manual)*

*(Check one)*

The purpose, function, and nonprofit status of this organization and the exempt status for Federal income tax purposes
[X] Have not changed during preceding 12 months
[ ] Have changed during preceding 12 months
*(If changed, publisher must submit explanation of change with this statement.)*

| 10. EXTENT AND NATURE OF CIRCULATION | AVERAGE NO. COPIES EACH ISSUE DURING PRECEDING 12 MONTHS | ACTUAL NUMBER OF COPIES OF SINGLE ISSUE PUBLISHED NEAREST TO FILING DATE |
|---|---|---|
| A. TOTAL NO. COPIES PRINTED *(Net Press Run)* | 65,000 | 65,000 |
| B. PAID CIRCULATION 1. SALES THROUGH DEALERS AND CARRIERS, STREET VENDORS AND COUNTER SALES | None | None |
| 2. MAIL SUBSCRIPTIONS | 62,200 | 62,200 |
| C. TOTAL PAID CIRCULATION | 49,200 | 49,200 |
| D. FREE DISTRIBUTION *(including samples)* BY MAIL, CARRIER OR OTHER MEANS | 13,000 | 13,000 |
| E. TOTAL DISTRIBUTION *(Sum of C and D)* | 62,200 | 62,200 |
| F. OFFICE USE, LEFT-OVER, UNACCOUNTED, SPOILED AFTER PRINTING | 2,800 | 2,800 |
| G. TOTAL *(Sum of E & F—should equal net press run shown in A)* | 65,000 | 65,000 |

I certify that the statements made by me above are correct and complete.

*(Signature of editor, publisher, business manager, or owner)* a Ray Appelquist

POD Form **3526** May 1968

# Thoughts of a Soldier in Vietnam

## By Jack Montgomery

The following unfinished letter was found in the personal belongings of Corporal Jack Montgomery and returned to his mother following his death from battle wounds last May. We wanted to share it with you.

IT IS DARK and I am near my foxhole on guard. There are flares exploding steadily so I can see enough to write a little. I got a letter from home last week. Mom said the church always remembers us in their prayers. Due to the situation here, I can tell you that there are no words I can find to express my appreciation for those prayers.

I have seen many pastors change over in that church. I remember when the roof seemed a hundred feet high and when I had to stand on tiptoe to see over the altar. It has always been my church.

The people there I have seen come and go, old and young, and I knew them all. And now I must thank all of you for remembering me.

There is one thing I would like to mention here. When you pray do not only ask God for safety, strength, and courage, but always remember to thank him for that which he has already given us. Everyday is Thanksgiving here. Every hour is Thanksgiving here. There are no atheists. I have met one man with agnostic views, but he is new and has not yet seen action. I'm sure he will change. For those back there who believe God is dead, send them here for awhile. You run into God every time you turn around.

Our Easter services were well worth telling about. We were camped in a graveyard. We had no chaplain so our squad got together for a brief service. We read of the resurrection and then prayed. It was very short and very simple, but I will never forget it.

The news from home has been of interest to us. The topic of peace talks, the president's decision not to run for re-election, but deepest

54

feelings came from the news of the assassination of Dr. Martin Luther King. I was under a poncho with three Negroes when we heard the news. We discussed it, not as three Negroes and one white man, but as four men. One made the remark that if the people back home could only see how we live together, work together, care for one another, over here, then there would be no consideration given to color.

Another incident which seemed remarkable to me occurred shortly after I arrived here. My fire-team leader, a large colored man from St. Louis, and I were on observation post near a school for students of Buddha. One student walked over to Baines and holding their wrists together pointed and laughed at the differences in color. Then he pointed at my wrist without laughing, Baines pointed to his own hand and said "Negro." He then pointed at my hand and said, "Caucasian." The Vietnamese student looked a little confused. Then Baines held our wrists together and said, "Both Americans." The student understood this. The simple words were perfect. I even seemed to understand a little better myself.

It is for us all that I hope you will pray. And if there are any among you who refuse to pray for a man because of his color, then write and tell me. I will pray for him.

I have listened to the words of you people for 20 years, and in every case I was able to profit from them. I am not a preacher, but if you will allow me to say a few words

about things which I have learned here, I would feel better. I know now that I always have taken the finer things of life for granted. There is little freedom here. After dark anyone who moves in rural areas is suspected of being VC and they are responded to accordingly. It is a cold way of doing it but it is necessary.

There is little electricity. The village huts have no windows or doors. Seldom do you see floors other than dirt. The sanitation problem is tremendous. It seems that all of the things we understand as necessities at home are no more than a distant hope for these people. They are kicked from house to house, taking refuge anywhere, as the war goes on around them. The VC move into a village. The people move out. We move in and obliterate the village. That is the common sequence.

Our town of Cabool has been well represented in this war. We have suffered, but we have suffered little in contrast to some places. We ask you to stand behind us. You hold the greatest, most effective weapon in this war. That is prayer. Remember us.

There are many who seldom hear from home. I have been lucky— friends and relatives have written regularly. But for those who seldom hear from home I wish there was something you could do just to let them know you are thinking of them. Not only the church but the entire town should join together in support. We think we are doing the right thing. Your encouragement would confirm our beliefs.

And for those who question our right of being here, I ask, Did the doughboys have the right to fight in Europe in 1917? Did we have the right to respond to the bombing of Pearl Harbor in 1941? Did we go wrong in defending Korea in the early '50s? The question is not whether we have the right. The question is do we have the responsibility. Isolationism is dangerous for a major power. I believe we have the responsibility.

Before long we will all be returning home, God willing. Again, you people will be interrupted in your night's sleep by the loud screeching tires on the pavement. You'll become annoyed and disgusted with this younger generation. It is true we are lively youth, but remember, we are young. Call us down when we need it. We don't deny we need it.

But here in Vietnam you never hear anyone say, "Why me?" We understand why. It is our time to live. We are the ones now who are responsible. Please remember when we come home that it is our time to live, and I will guarantee we all will live better for we have seen a life without freedom.

And also, in your prayers, please remember all the boys in uniform, regardless of location. There are many who fail to receive proper credit for their work only because they are not here. Without them our work here could not possibly function. Remember them for they do as much as we do...  ■■

## Notes from Uppsala
(continued from page 26)

shock of assassinations, the tumult and revolt of students, the clash of race and greed.

"Can it come off?" Dr. Blake asked. In his closing remarks to the Assembly, Dr. Blake acknowledged: "Uppsala turned the churches from inside to the outside, from ecclesiastical business to mission and service to the world. It was not as conservative as predicted, and more ecumenical than expected."  ■■

## He Sought the Secrets of the Pole
(continued from page 43)

To strive, to seek, to find, but not to yield.

Twenty-two years later, England, thinking of Scott, built the first polar museum in the world. Across the front of the building they inscribed a dedication to their dead hero. The translation from Latin reads: "He sought the secrets of the Pole. He found the secrets of God."

Although Scott lost the race, he was more than a winner. For thousands have been inspired by his example.  ■■

Like Father, Like Son
I meant to teach my son
Not to procrastinate;
But I found I had left it
Until it was too late.
—Harold L. Taylor

56

# A Marriage Should Start Off Right

## By Ruth E. Temple

WAR, as always, brings all kinds of people together in all kinds of places. This is a true story of a recent incident in a small North Carolina town.

It was early morning and Sarah, a retired schoolteacher, was sweeping the sidewalk in front of her home. A car driven by a young man in khaki stopped opposite her. She noticed a girl sitting beside the boy as he leaned out of the car window and spoke.

"Ma'am, can you direct us to a Justice of the Peace? We want to get married."

"You don't want a Justice of the Peace," said Sarah. "You want a minister and I can tell you just where to find one."

"Thank you, but we haven't time. We are in a hurry."

Sarah didn't give up that easily. "It won't take any longer to be married by a minister. A Justice of the Peace office is no place for you to get married."

"No, thank you." The boy was firm. "Will you tell me where I can find the JP?"

Sarah directed him to the office of the Justice and went into the house. "Jane," she said to her sister, "did you see that boy I was talking to? He had a girl with him and they were looking for a Justice of the Peace to marry them. I tried to talk the boy into going to a minister, but I got nowhere. I know Mr. Wilson would be glad to help them."

"Yes, I saw him. It's a pity. They looked like a real nice couple and you know what that JP's office looks like."

As she spoke, the doorbell sounded. It was the soldier boy back again. He introduced himself and the girl who was with him. "You were right. We can't get married in that place. Will you please tell me where we can find a minister?"

Mary, the girl explained: "You see, James has only one week before he'll be sent overseas to Vietnam. We wanted to have just a simple little wedding in the chapel with only my pastor, my family, and James' family there. My mother wouldn't agree; she insisted on a big wedding in the church sanctuary, preparations for which would take up all our time, and we could not talk her out of it. So last night, James and I packed our bags and left. We've driven all night—we're from New Jersey—and this looked like a nice quiet little town to be married in. Do you understand? I do hope you do."

Jane and Sarah both assured the couple that they did and sympathized fully. "You want to start your marriage off right, I'm sure," said Jane. "Let Sarah show you where the minister lives and after you are married, come back here. We'll all have a cup of coffee together to celebrate. You remind me of my granddaughter, Mary; she's engaged to a soldier, too."

"Thank you so much," said James and Mary together. Sarah went with them and they found the minister in his study. When the situation was explained to him, Mr. Wilson readily cooperated. The marriage ceremony was performed in a small chapel in the church building and the minister closed with a tender prayer for James' safety and the future happiness of the young couple. Mrs. Wilson and Sarah served as witnesses to the marriage.

Jane had coffee and cookies ready when the three returned. While the others ate, Sarah went to her room and returned with a small gift. It was wrapped in white tissue paper

and tied with white ribbon. "Something for your future home," she explained. Jane had already wrapped a jar of her homemade damson jelly, which she presented. James and Mary tried to say thank-you but their grateful looks said more than their halting words.

When they said goodbye to the sisters, James and Mary kissed both of them. James said, "We'll always remember you," and Mary added, "I'm so glad we were persuaded to have a minister marry us. We'll never forget his beautiful prayer especially for us. Thank you again so much, and goodbye." ■■

## TO BE SURE

"The trouble with some people," the principal told his secretary, "is that they don't admit their faults. I'd admit mine—if I had any."—*Mississippi Educational Advance.*

### Testimony from Iowa Governor Harold E. Hughes

"I am an alcoholic," said Iowa Governor Harold E. Hughes in a talk at the 28th International Congress on Alcohol and Alcoholism at the Shoreham Hotel, Washington, D. C. "I was born an alcoholic. I never took a normal drink in my life. I realized that, for me, to drink was to die. I could not drink and maintain sobriety."

Once a truck driver, the 46-year-old governor said he gave up drinking 14 years ago.

58

# Brief News Items

## Correspondence Course on Theology

The Rev. Robt. P. Bollman, of the Christ Episcopal Church in La Crosse, Wis., has developed a correspondence course in theology especially for military personnel. He writes: "This course is geared to anyone who wants a good solid course in Scripture, theology, and comparative Christian religions. It is available free of charge (with the exception of a self-addressed envelope). The course is open to military personnel and APOs if proper postage is put on the return envelope. We have tried to make this a course with more 'guts.' We expect that people who begin the course will do one lesson a week for 50 weeks or whatever their schedule allows."

## Return to the Bible

During National Bible Week, last October 20 to 27, emphasis was placed by 100 businessmen in America across the country on a "return to the Bible." Reading the Scriptures was never more needed in the nation's life than today, these men declared.

**Two young men of the Overseas Crusades, Inc. presented a musical program and message at Naha Wheel Chapel, Okinawa. L-R: Chaplain (CPT) Raymond A. Acker, Protestant Chaplain, greets Mike Yakenelli, Youth for Christ Director, San Diego, Calif., and Chuck Ohman, Minister of Music for Highland Park Baptist Church, Detroit, Mich.**

"Sunday Afternoon on the Rectory Lawn" is an innovation to give Basic Cadets at the U.S. Air Force Academy an opportunity to visit the Rectories and meet the Cadet Chaplains of all three faiths. They were welcomed by the Command Chaplain and given refreshments which was followed by a musical program at which many church and civic choral groups from the local area have participated.

### Have Bible—Will Travel

Replacement personnel coming to the 1st Air Cavalry Division are all given refresher training in the basic principles of combat and operational concepts of air mobility. The classes are conducted by the division training center located at the base of Hong Kong Mountain in the central highlands of Vietnam.

Most important during this four-day period is the chaplain's visit. Worship services are available to all who choose. And chaplains may be seen in any remote section where the men are fighting.—From M/Sgt. Ernest C. Bradley, IE 1st Air Cav. Div. APO San Francisco 96490.

### He Wants a Harmonica

Will you please send this letter on to the New York Free and Accepted Order of Masons. I'd like to receive one of their harmonicas. (Re your article in September, 1968). I always wanted to learn to play one and this will be the best time since I am over here away from my family and "peace will prevail" in learning. Ha!

SFC Otis O. Gaskin, RA 55006202, HHC 15th SS Bn, 1st Air Cav. Div. APO SF, Calif. 96490.

*We sent Otis' letter on to the Grand Lodge in N.Y. and they replied: We have been sending gift packages for mass distribution to military units and military hospitals in Vietnam. Harmonicas and instruction books are included in our 70-pound packages. We are not geared to sending gifts to individual servicemen. However, because the request that came to you was triggered by your article on harmonicas, we are sending to SFC Otis G. Gaskin a harmonica and instruction book. We can report to you that the responses we have received from servicemen, chaplains, and commanding officers encourage us in our program.—* Dr. Edward J. Lowy, Grand Lodge Free and Accepted Masons of the State of New York, 71 W. 23rd St., New York, N. Y. 10010.

## PHOTO CREDITS

Page 9, Lee MacDonald; pages 19, 21, 22, World Council of Churches; page 38, British Museum; page 41, Library of Congress; page 42, U.S. Coast Guard; page 59, U.S. Army; page 60, U.S. Air Force; page 61, SHAPE.

*Above*: General Lyman L. Lemnitzer, Supreme Allied Commander Europe, presents the symbolic key of the SHAPE Chapel Center to International Staff Chaplain (COL) Herman N. Benner, during Dedication Ceremonies, SHAPE, Belgium. *Below*: SHAPE Choral Society under Dr. Francois Kerremans provided the music for the dedication program.

# The Link Calendar

**Jan. 1.** New Year's Day. Football games (Rose, Orange, Sugar, Cotton, etc.). Parades (including Mummers'). On this day in 1863, President Abraham Lincoln signed the Emancipation Proclamation.

**Jan. 2.** On this day in 1788 Georgia ratified the Constitution.

**Jan. 3.** E. Stanley Jones, eminent American missionary and writer, was born on this day in 1884.

**Jan. 4.** Birthday of St. Titus; feast of St. Titus. Sir Isaac Newton born on this day in 1642.

**Jan. 5.** 2nd Sunday in Christmastide.

**Jan. 6.** Epiphany. The 12th Day After Christmas. The Four Freedoms (of speech and expression; to worship God in his own way; from want; from fear). On this day in 1941 enunciated by Franklin D. Roosevelt.

**Jan. 7.** Millard Fillmore, 13th Pres of the U.S., born this day in 1800.

**Jan. 8.** Battle of New Orleans, 1815.

**Jan. 11.** Alexander Hamilton. Born this day in 1757.

**Jan. 12.** First Sunday after Epiphany.

**Jan. 14.** Albert Schweitzer born this day in 1875.

**Jan. 19.** Second Sunday after Epiphany. Jan. 19-26. Church and Economic Life Week. Also birthday of Robert E. Lee, b. 1807. Also birthday of Edgar Allen Poe, b. on this day in 1809.

**Jan. 20.** Inauguration Day.

**Jan. 21.** "Stonewall" Jackson. Born this day in 1824.

**Jan. 24.** Gold discovered in California this day in 1848. Also on this day the first Boy Scout troop organized in England—1908.

**Jan. 25.** Robert Burns born this day in 1759... It is an old belief that the weather of the whole year depends upon this day.

**Jan. 26.** Third Sunday after Epiphany. On this day in 1880 was born General Douglas MacArthur.

**Jan. 29.** William McKinley, 25th President of the U.S., born this day in 1843.

**Jan. 30.** Franklin D. Roosevelt, 32nd President of the U.S. Born this day in 1882.

**Jan. 31.** Child Labor Day. For suggested programs write National Child Labor Committee, 419 4th Ave., New York City.

QUOTES: It takes the storm to prove the real shelter.—*Construction Digest*.

SIGN ON LAWN OF CHURCH IN BOSTON: Life is Fragile. Handle with Prayer.

WIFE TO NEIGHBORLY LADY: "Al really has only one fault. He can't seem to do anything right."—Gene Yasenak.

LUCK is always against the man who depends on it.—*Sunshine Magazine*.

# *Discussion Helps*

THROUGHOUT this issue of THE LINK, you will find four articles prepared not only for individual reading, but also for group discussion and for lay leaders' helps.

1. **You've Got to Run Risks** *(page 5)*
   *Biblical Material*: Mark 8:34-38

   In Mark 8:34, what did Jesus mean by "cross"? What is the cross you should take up now? What is the difference between "risk" and "gamble"? Is the Christian faith a gamble? If not, why not? We say "run risks" yet we also sing "How Firm a Foundation," how do you reconcile these two dimensions of Christian experience?

2. **Jericho Road Philosophies** *(page 27)*
   *Biblical Material*: Luke 10:25-37

   What philosophies of life are revealed in the story of the good Samaritan? Cite examples where each of these philosophies has been practiced. Why is Jesus like the good Samaritan?

3. **Abraham: Man Without a Road Map** *(page 32)*
   *Biblical Material*: Genesis 12:1-9; 17:1-8; 22:1-19

   Why do we call Abraham "a man without a road map"? Why did God call Abraham to "get thee out"? What was the covenant God made with Abraham? What does the story of Abraham's willingness to offer up Isaac teach us?

4. **God Enough and Enough God for Me** *(page 50)*
   *Biblical Material*: John 1:1-13

   What do we learn from Jesus about God? Why is it said that the man of deepest faith experiences "the dark night of the soul"? To what extent does God disclose himself to man? What is the meaning of the incarnation? How is Jesus "the light of the world"?

QUOTES: When you start feeling critical of the human race, just remember

# Books Are Friendly Things

**Vocabulary Power. A New, Step-by-Step Guide to Total Word Mastery** by Edward L. Tucker. Bantam Books, Inc. 271 Madison Ave., New York, N. Y. 1968. 75 cents.

The view of this text is that the simplest way to improve your vocabulary is to give you a few new words each week to learn thoroughly. This book therefore contains 240 carefully chosen words and exercises by which you learn these words. And you can do one exercise in 30 minutes. An excellent guide toward word mastery.

**Why Be a Christian?** by Rosemary Haughton. J. B. Lippincott Co., East Washington Sq., Philadelphia, Pa. 19105. 1968. $3.95.

Almost everyone asks this question during his lifetime. Mrs. Haughton, Roman Catholic laywoman (also author, illustrator, and mother of ten), presents her reasons in this penetrating book. To be a Christian, one must know what a Christian is. In what way are all Christians similar? Different? Rosemary Haughton says that you come into a true relationship with God through sincere belief, and because God has called you to proclaim the good news in truth, which should be heard in faith and answered by love.

**Sherlock Holmes' Greatest Cases.** Edited by Howard Haycraft. Bantam Books, Inc., 271 Madison Ave., New York, N. Y. 10016. 1968. 95 cents.

After an introduction by Haycraft on Arthur Conan Doyle, the writer, and Sherlock Holmes, the fiction master detective that Doyle created, this book contains a novel and six short stories in which Holmes is the hero. Doyle imparted a unique reality to the character, Sherlock Holmes. To this day hundreds of letters and appeals for help have been addressed with touching faith to the man who never lived—Sherlock Holmes, 221B, Baker Street, London.

**John Knox** by Jasper Ridley. Oxford University, 200 Madison Ave., New York, N. Y. 10016. 1968. $9.50.

Once Mary, Queen of Scots, said: "I fear the prayers of John Knox more than the swords of 10,000 men." Ridley has written a thorough and magnificent biography about the spiritual leader of Scotland who lived from 1514 to 1572. The author says of Knox: "Knox is one of the most ruthless and successful revolutionary leaders in history."

64

# Sound Off!   (Continued from page 4)

my office as well as my friends in the states and in this command have all told me how much they've enjoyed reading the article about me in your magazine.

—Link S. White, Information Officer, U. S. Army Supt Comd., Da Nang (Prov). APO San Francisco 96349.

### THE LINK Is Much Appreciated

I still read THE LINK as faithfully as ever, and I know I speak for many, many thousands when I say how much a magazine like THE LINK is needed and appreciated in the military. We get quite a quantity here, as you probably know. My mother is bringing out a book of poetry and would like to use in it some of the poems she has published in THE LINK.

—TSgt Marlin W. Helmick, Chaplain Services Superintendent, Hq. Sq. Sec. LTTC, Lowry AFB, CO 80230.

### How Get THE LINK in the Philippines?

I respectfully request information whether subscription of your monthly magazine THE LINK could be extended to the Philippines. I am presently a member of a military contingent, 1st Phil Civic Action Group, stationed in Vietnam. And our overseas may subsequently be terminated in the near future and there should subscription be granted while here in Vietnam, I have also the intention to extend this in our homeland.

For your information, I have just taken hold of your magazine, issue May '68 by total accident. And as I have read the first article entitled "God and Sex," immediately aroused my interest. It is very educational and enlightenment spiritually. Undoubtedly there are more interesting articles in this issue and expect same in the future.

—T/Sgt D. S. Lagda, Sta Hosp 1st Phillagy, Tay Ninh, South Vietnam

*(Sgt Lagda has received our letter—we hope. We do have bases in the Philippines that receive THE LINK and we would be glad to hear from other groups out there. Send us an order for any number of copies and we will mail THE LINK. Copies go all over the world.—EDITOR.)*

### From a Contributor

Please let me take a moment to thank you for your purchases of humor items for THE LINK and THE CHAPLAIN magazines which you so capably edit. I am, of course, thanking you also in behalf of my wife—Anna Herbert. We are both appreciative of your having your staff mail copies of your publications which we enjoy and are proud to be part of them.

—Jack Herbert, 1350 Astor St., Chicago, Ill. 60610.

# At Ease!

"I enjoyed tonight, Jerome. All two dollars of it."

The following story is making the rounds in Prague: A distinguished Czechoslovakian economist, just returned from a visit to the U.S., met a friend in a cafe. "What did you study in the U. S.?" asked the friend. "I went to study the death of capitalism," replied the economist. The friend then asked: "How did you find it?" Replied the economist with a sigh: "What a wonderful way to die." — *U. S. News and World Report.*

Skitch: What's that you have in your buttonhole?

Mitch: That's a chrysanthemum.

Skitch: Looks like a rose to me.

Mitch: Nope, it's a chrysanthemum.

Skitch: Whaddya mean? Spell it.

Mitch: K-R-I-S...by golly, it *is* a rose!

He: I loved a girl once, and she made a fool out of me.

She: Well, some girls really leave a lasting impression! — *Builders.*

Norman Allen (of Prestonsburg, Ky.) overheard this conversation while a woman was taking her exam for a driver's license.

"What is the white line for in the middle of the road?" asked the state trooper.

"That," she replied positively, "is for bicycles." — AP.

"So you're lost, little man," said the lady, "Why didn't you hang on to your mother's skirt?"

Answered the youngster: "Couldn't reach it!" — *Woodmen of the World Magazine.*

Preparing to give a small boy an aptitude test, a psychiatrist told his nurse to put a pitchfork, wrench, and hammer on a table. "If he grabs the pitchfork, he'll be a farmer. If he grabs the wrench he'll be a mechanic. If he grabs the hammer, he'll be a carpenter." But the kid fooled everyone. He grabbed the nurse. — *Lion.*

### Friendship's Brand

A smile which drives the clouds away,
Kind words which saves for me the day,
A lift for which I cannot pay,
A faith which makes me want to pray,
    Brands you a friend.

      —Osa Webb

### Marking the Calendar

Each day
is one day
closer to the
day my soldier man
comes back across
the waters
to me.

—Viola Jacobson Berg

CPSIA information can be obtained
at www.ICGtesting.com
Printed in the USA
BVHW040908050219
539516BV00009B/163/P

9 780483 600973